HOW TO CHOOSE A MATE

HOW TO CHOOSE A MATE

Mavis Klein

MARION BOYARS
LONDON · BOSTON

First published in the United States in 1981
by Marion Boyars Publishers Inc
99 Main Street, Salem, New Hampshire 03079
First published in Great Britain in 1981
by Marion Boyars Publishers Ltd
18 Brewer Street, London W1R 4AS

Australian distribution by Thomas C. Lothian
4-12 Tattersalls Lane, Melbourne, Victoria 3000

British Library Cataloguing in Publication Data

Klein, Mavis
How to choose a mate.
1. Marriage 2. Personality
I. Title
301.42'7 HQ734 80-40918

ISBN 0-7145-2727-0

Library of Congress Catalog Card Number 80-40918

Typeset by John Smith, London
Printed in Great Britain by
REDWOOD BURN LIMITED
Trowbridge & Esher

For my future sons-in-law

CONTENTS

INTRODUCTION

Choosing the right partner can lead to the happiest and most rewarding of human relationships. To love and be loved, to be understood deeply, to have someone to depend on, to share interests and do things together, to share joy and sorrow is the fulfilment of human longing. Yet happy marriages are rare. Thirty to forty per cent of marriages in the West end in divorce and most of the rest are unsatisfactory relationships held together for a variety of reasons.

There are many causes of unhappy relationships, but we often use a single blanket explanation – 'incompatibility'. What many people do not realize is that the elements of incompatibility that eventually cause the breakdown of a relationship were there from the beginning. When a once loving and joyous relationship turns sour and miserable, as well as hurting us and making us unhappy, we are often puzzled and confused. Especially if it all began as 'being in love', a state of being which most of us are encouraged to believe is the ideal basis for a relationship, we ask ourselves why love has failed us and what hope we can sensibly have that it will not fail us again in a future, new relationship. We search for causes in external circumstances beyond our control and in the 'unreasonableness' of our partner's attitudes or behaviour, but few people ever question their over-riding assumption that the relationship was begun with only happiness in mind.

The truth, incomprehensible and unpalatable as it may at first seem, is that we all actually seek unhappiness as well as happiness. Without realizing it, from the beginning, we are as deeply attracted to the negative attributes as to the positive attributes of the person we love. Later, we may say, 'But I didn't know then that he would develop a drink problem,' or, 'I didn't know then that she would be unfaithful'. Yet incredibly frequently the wife whose husband becomes an alcoholic had an alcoholic father and the husband of the faithless wife had a faithless mother. Each of us is driven by unconscious compulsions to repeat our original family experiences – even when we are *consciously* trying to do the opposite. Which of us can honestly claim never to mess things up while aiming for perfection, never to make more haste for less speed, never to try too hard to succeed – and thus fail – never to put our foot in it while intending to be solicitous of another, or never to set things up for ourselves to be rebuffed when what we want most of all is to be accepted? All these everyday occurrences are instances of our unconscious selves winning over our conscious selves in seeking some form of misery, however minor.

The aim of this book is to help people, through enabling them to gain awareness of all parts of themselves, more surely to choose overall joy rather than overall misery in their relationships and in all the rest of their lives as well.

Compatibility of human personalities is not a simple thing to define, and there are many factors – some more important than others – involved. Acknowledging the relevant realities requires absolute honesty on both sides and a willingness to talk freely about everything, including delicate and sometimes painful matters.

INTRODUCTION

Hundreds of thousands of people seek partners in a multitude of advertisements in the press of almost every country in the world. Marriage and friendship bureaux may charge exhorbitant fees for an introduction, but their success rates are very low because all they do is introduce people whom they judge, very superficially, to be of interest to one another, and there their responsibility ends.

Choosing a partner, whether for a casual relationship or a more serious one, entails making a decision and, as with all decisions, several factors are involved. What do you need? What do you want? What are the alternatives? How much information do I need about him or her? What are the future possibilities? These are what this book is about.

The aim is to help the reader understand her- or himself, to assess his or her true needs, and to discover what type of person would be most likely to fulfil those needs. But this is only one part of the relationship, for (s)he will also have to find out the needs of the other person and whether or not (s)he can fulfil them.

The theory of human nature used in this book is Transactional Analysis, developed in the 1950's by the late Dr. Eric Berne, and made famous by his best-seller *Games People Play*, first published in 1964.

Like most present-day theories of personality, TA – as Transactional Analysis is familiarly called – takes for granted the now commonplace assumptions about human nature which are, in fact, the heritage of Freud. The most central of these assumptions is that our adult personalities and characters are directly determined – albeit largely unconsciously – by our experiences in the first few years of our lives. While the importance of heredity is not denied, our early life experiences are seen as the predominant cause of the overall quality of our lives thereafter. Heredity defines the limits – the child born to parents who are both six-footers has a much better chance of becoming a high-jumper (if he wants to) than the child born to parents who are both five foot two. But within the bounds defined by heredity there is much scope for the variables in the environment to exert their power also – improved nutrition has made many young adults today outstrip both their parents in height and overall physical robustness. So, too, in matters of psychology, although compared with the physical influences of our early environments the psychological influences are often much subtler and more covert.

Inasmuch as TA expounds the above understanding as its own core tenet, it is not different from any of the wide variety of theories of personality that are direct descendants of psychoanalysis. Yet each contemporary theory has its own particular vocabulary in which it expresses generally accepted psychoanalytic wisdom, and each theoretical vocabulary tends to bring into focus and emphasize different aspects of reality. The core concept in TA is 'ego states' – the Parent, the Adult and the Child. These are not roles, but *states of being*, amongst which we switch, hour by hour, minute by minute, and second by second during all of our waking lives. Each ego state contains its own impulses and attitudes which may not be – and often are not – consistent or even compatible with the impulses and attitudes of the other two.

All three ego states are needed for effective functioning in everyday life and none is 'better' or 'worse' than either of the others. But different situations are more *appropriately* dealt with by one ego state rather than another, and TA makes sense of much everyday irritability with ourselves and most misunderstandings between people in terms of our inappropriate use of one ego state when another is needed. In the past twenty years or so the use of TA in therapeutic, educational and business settings in the United States – and increasingly elsewhere – has demonstrated unambiguously that knowledge of ego states is capable of vastly enhancing an individual's sense of his own well-being as well as the effectiveness of his interactions with others.

The vocabulary of TA – which includes such terms as 'strokes', 'messages' and 'permissions' as well as the core Parent, Adult and Child ego states – is singular in the precision, concision and lucidity by which it enables even very young children to understand and use profound psychological concepts which were previously elusive in the everyday consciousness of most people.

New, successful applications of TA continue to be found, and it is hoped *How to Choose a Mate* is one of them. Each chapter consists of an introductory summary of the ideas contained in the chapter, followed by an elaboration of those ideas, which includes questions intended to help readers apply the ideas to understanding their own personalities and relationships.

CHAPTER ONE

Being Human

All human beings have three basic characteristics in common. The total 'self' of each human being is made up of separate, smaller 'selves' called *ego states*. These are our *feeling self*, our *thinking self*, and our *believing self*. The second characteristic all human beings share is our lifelong need to be *'stroked'*. A stroke is any act of recognition given by one person to another. The most fundamental kind of stroke is – as the word implies – voluntary physical contact made by one person with another, but all other gestures, including speech, through which one person acknowledges the existence of another, are also strokes. So our need for strokes refers both to our need for physical contact with others and to our psychological need to be recognized and responded to by others. Thirdly, all human beings have a built-in need to *make sense of the world and of relationships*, that is, to experience the physical world and our relationships to other people as ordered and more or less predictable rather than chaotic and unpredictable.

Our feeling self is called our Child ego state, our thinking self is called our Adult ego state, and our believing self is called our Parent ego state. Our need for strokes is, in infancy, literally the need to be physically stroked, but, later on, words and other symbolic substitutes can fulfil this basic need. We learn to make sense of relationships by interacting with people, especially through our interactions with our immediate family in the early months and years of life. By the age of about six, we have all our ego states, we know how to get strokes, and our practical understanding of the physical world and of human relationships is highly developed.

EGO STATES

Once the reality of the three different ego states is accepted, it becomes immediately clear that the commonsense idea that each of us has one 'real self' is false. Yet accepting the anti-commonsense idea of three different 'selves' in each of us makes much more sense in terms of our everyday experience of life. Consider how often in everyday life you have difficulty making up your mind – how often you need to weigh many factors in the balance before you confidently make a choice of action, or pass judgement on something or somebody, or compromise between your own wishes and your sense of responsibility to others.

All such problems arise because our total 'self' is made up of smaller, separate, independent ego states. Sometimes these ego states all agree with each other and then we feel fine; but at least as often as not our Parent, Adult and Child ego states battle with each other and we have to work hard to make peace between them.

Dr. Eric Berne, the founder of Transactional Analysis, was the first psychologist to emphasize the importance of recognizing and naming the different ego states that make up a whole person. Getting to understand ourselves and others in terms of ego states will be the main focus of this book, but for the time being suffice it to say that our Parent usually looks and acts like mothers and fathers often do, our Adult looks sensible and acts rationally, and our Child looks emotional and acts expressively, as children usually do. It is often convenient to represent our three ego states diagrammatically, as below.

Having these three ego states is the first characteristic that all human beings have in common.

STROKES

The second characteristic that all human beings have in common is the *need for strokes*. In the first place, when we are babies, this need is quite literal. The loving skin to skin contact that parents give their babies is as vital to their survival as food. And this is no exaggeration. During the 1940's the psychologist Renée Spitz, investigating the high death rate of babies in a particular orphanage, discovered that all the babies were kept clean and well-fed and had no discernible physical disease. Yet many lost weight and seemed simply to 'waste away', sometimes to the point of death. Spitz identified the one vital element that was lacking in these babies' lives – an abundance of close physical contact in a loving and intimate relationship with one other person, who is usually, but not necessarily, a baby's mother. However, the vast majority of us are more fortunate. Most parents instinctively give their babies all the tender loving *physical stroking* that is so vital to their well-being, and most babies grow and thrive. A contented baby held lovingly in its mother's arms is often depicted as the epitome of bliss, and there is a great deal of psychological evidence that deep in the unconscious part of our Child this is the state of being we all long to return to.

In reality, of course, this nirvana can no longer be had once infancy is past. The closest we get to it again is in *loving sexual intimacy*, which for most grown-ups is the most sought-after and fulfilling of all possible experiences. But even this is not enough. Our stroke needs are continuous and imperative throughout the whole of our lives and even people passionately in love cannot fulfil *all* of each other's stroke needs. And, anyhow, what of people who do not achieve such blissful relationships in their grown-up lives? And what of children who, once past infancy, are every day less and less rocked and stroked in somebody's arms? Must we all live on a starvation diet of strokes except when passionately in love?

The answer lies in the fact that human beings are *symbolic creatures*. Unlike other species, we are *psychological as well as biological beings*, and are thus capable of getting our stroke needs met in much more subtle and indirect ways than by more or less continuous physical contact with other human beings. We talk to each other, expressing in words, affection, appreciation, admiration, gratitude, sympathy, pleasure in each others' company. We also 'say it with flowers' and in many other symbolic gestures, all of which have the power to make us feel as contented as if we were being physically stroked.

True, even in these terms it is possible to be stroke-deprived – and many people are. That is why it is so important for people to realize how basic and lifelong their need for strokes is. Becoming aware of our needs is often more than half the battle won in getting those needs fulfilled.

MAKING SENSE OF LIFE

The third characteristic that all human beings have in common is the *need to make sense of the world and of ourselves in relation to the world and to other people.*

A newborn infant in his earliest days of being alive almost certainly has only the single inchoate experience of the world as a buzzing, whirring confusion. The only distinctions he can make are those of overall satisfaction – in which case he is either feeding or asleep – or overall pain – in which case he is crying and throbbing in every fibre of his being. He does not seem capable even of distinguishing between 'self' and 'not self'. He and the universe are one.

But step by step, to the delight and awesome wonder of most parents, through the use of faculties built into his brain, the baby begins to *know things.* By about a month he can focus his eyes and a single object can be seen by him as separate from the totality of everything in his field of vision. By about six months of age he clearly demonstrates that he knows the difference between 'self' and 'not self'; he can reach for and hold and drop an object and cry for it when it is out of reach. And from this time onward his knowledge of the physical realities of life increases by leaps and bounds. He learns that if his body comes into too rapid or forceful contact with an object 'it hurts'. He learns that hot things hurt, too. He learns that 'what goes up must come down'. He learns that some things are heavy and some things light and that some things too heavy to lift can be moved by horizontal force. He learns that an object on wheels can be given added momentum with friction and that objects vary in their fragility. Until, by about the age of four, his *practical knowledge of the laws of physics* is virtually complete.

Alongside all the knowledge he gains in these few years about *physical reality* he acquires an equivalent amount of *knowledge of psychological reality*. At about six weeks of age he knows that human faces bring him pleasure, and he proves he knows this with a stroke-inducing smile. By about two months of age he knows his mother's face as distinct from all faces as promising the most strokes of all, and by about seven months he probably responds to the *absence* of his mother with terror. He is beginning to experience what stroke-deprivation means. By about nine months he knows cunning ways to get attention – that is strokes, if they are not forthcoming – such as by banging his spoon on his high-chair tray when his mother is paying attention – that is giving strokes – to someone other than himself. Until, by about six years of age, from his experiences of family life, he *knows* all the essentials of psychological reality – *that is the meaning of strokes and how to get them.*

Although the six-year-old has only a very limited capacity for expressing in *words* (either in her own mind or in talking to others) what she knows about the world and about human relationships, by the evidence of her *actions* she already has vast stores of information and wisdom. Indeed, not only six-year-olds but all grown-ups, too, are rarely self-conscious of all the learning we once had to do that enables us now to manage our lives at even the simplest levels.

Most of the time we take for granted our everyday effectiveness, calling it 'instinctive'. Only structural engineers, in their everyday working lives, may need to be fully aware of the laws of physics; and only psychotherapists need, in their working lives, to be fully aware of the differences between people caused by the variability in people's early family ralationships. Yet all normal people respect the Law of Gravity, know the dangers of cars, live wires and fires, can cut their own toe nails, adroitly handle a knife and fork and . . . a thousand and one other things which once, long ago, before they *learnt*, they did not understand and could not do.

Similarly, all normal people – from about six years old onward – *know*, usually without being self-conscious of their knowledge, probably hundreds and maybe thousands of bits of information concerning effective interaction with other people. Much of this knowledge is ritualistic, such as saying 'hello' and 'goodbye', 'please' and 'thank-you', controlling our impulses to kick, push, spit or shout at other people in order to get what we want, and generally being obedient to the Golden Rule. Such ritualistic knowledge about effective interactions with other people is, for most people, as automatic and 'instinctive' as their knowledge that it is necessary to look both ways before crossing a road in order to save one's life. But at a deeper level than ritual we each have also acquired by the time we are about six an enormous amount of highly idiosyncratic knowledge about human relationships, which has been learnt in the intimate setting of our family life. By and large everyone's experiential knowledge of the physical world is identical with everybody else's, but there are very marked differences in the *psychological realities* exhibited in different families and therefore marked differences between what children in one family are taught compared with what children in another family are taught.

For instance, some children, by example and by precept, learn that having good manners is very important in getting on with others, some learn the value of keeping one's feelings to oneself, some learn that getting on with others is a struggle, some learn to expect hostility and to withdraw from others, some learn to demand of themselves and others scrupulous honesty in word and deed. Although in any particular culture there will always be considerable overlap between one person and another in their *learned ideas* about getting on with (that is, the best ways to get strokes from) others, there are also many differences between people in what they believe about human relationships. But it is usually only when communication between people results in obvious misunderstandings that we are made aware that *our* 'truth' about relationships is by no means identical with everybody else's truths.

Irrespective however of the variability of learned psychological knowledge, we need to acquire such knowledge in order to fulfil our underlying need to experience life as orderly and predictable. So, by the time a child is about six years old his basic personality is complete. His Parent, Adult and Child *ego states* are differentiated and available for their appropriate uses; experientially, he is aware of his and others' fundamental need for *strokes*; he moves about comfortably in the physical world because he knows enough about it to be confident of the *predictability of events* in response to his actions; and he moves about comfortably in the psychological world – at least amongst his family – because he knows enough about *how to get strokes* to make sure this most vital of his needs is fulfilled.

CHAPTER TWO

Being an Individual

Although all human beings have in common the three ego states, Parent, Adult and Child, people are different from each other in the *proportions* of each ego state that go to make up their 'whole selves'. While extreme dominance of one ego state is unhealthy, a certain degree of imbalance between ego states makes for healthy individuality. People are also different from each other in their typical ways of giving and getting strokes. There are nine different ways in which one person may give another a stroke. These nine ways of giving a stroke are the nine ways in which one of the three ego states of one person may address one of the three ego states of another person. These are Parent to Parent, Adult to Adult, Child to Child, Parent to Adult, Parent to Child, Adult to Parent,

Adult to Child, Child to Adult and Child to Parent. *Positive* strokes are strokes that make us feel good, *negative* strokes are strokes that make us feel bad, but our need for strokes is so great that we would rather get negative strokes than no strokes at all. Each person has her own favourite positive and negative stokes, called her *target strokes.* A person's positive target stroke is the stroke that makes her feel especially good about herself; her negative target stroke is the stroke that makes her feel especially bad about herself. People are also different from each other in the ways in which they make sense of life. While we all have the same basic undertanding of the *physical* world, we each have our own unique ways of making sense of the *psychological* world. Most people go through life mistakenly believing that other people's psychological reality is the same as their own.

HOW MUCH OF EACH EGO STATE?

The Parent, Adult and Child ego states in each individual together make up his or her 'whole self'. But although everybody is made up of these same basic components, most people have *unequal amounts of energy* in each of their ego states. Some people have such noticeably different proportions of Parent, Adult and Child in their make-up that we recognize them as distinct *types.*

The Parent Type. The person whose total self is dominated by his Parent ego state is basically guided by his *beliefs.* (S)he is very caring towards other people, but a bit on the bossy side as well. Such people put their moral principles above all else and look at life in terms of 'right versus wrong' and 'good versus bad'. They are honest, kind, reliable, solid citizens. They are unlikely ever to try to get away with not paying their bus fare and are marvellous in a crisis. They usually respond unhesitatingly to any situation because they unswervingly 'know' what is right to do, so others tend to feel secure in their presence. They often seem older than they are.

Parent-type people are fond of words like 'should' and 'shouldn't', 'must' and 'mustn't, 'always' and 'never', and aphorisms like: 'As you make your bed, so you lie on it.' They are both nurturing and critical or controlling towards other people. Other people tend to respond to them with compliance and respect or angry rebelliousness.

The Adult Type. The person whose total self is dominated by her Adult ego state is basically *unemotional.* These people are very rational and fair in their dealings with others, but their lack of emotion makes them cold. Such people are usually clear-headed, practical and knowledgeable. They are intelligent conversationalists and are marvellous in a situation that calls for weighing up the pros and cons. They pride themselves in being uninvolved.

Adult-type people are fond of words like 'how', 'what', 'when', 'possible', 'interesting' and 'be reasonable'. They are impatient with other people who allow their emotions to interfere with logic. Other people tend to seek them out for some specific purpose, such as their professional knowledge, but otherwise find them boring.

The Child Type. The person whose total self is dominated by his Child ego state is basically *impulsive.* These people respond to life in accordance with their feelings of the moment. Usually they are excitable, nervous, charming and fun-loving, but quite unreliable and inconsiderate of other people's wishes and needs. They are in their element at a party. They often seem younger than they are.

Child-type people are fond of words like 'wow', 'want', 'can't', 'won't', 'wish', 'hope' and 'I have a feeling that . . .' They tend to manipulate other people. When they are in a good mood they only want to be with people willing to be in the same mood with them; when they are in a bad mood, they demand that other people nurture and indulge them.

Other people tend to respond to them with love or hate.

As can be seen from the above description of the three extreme types of people, none of these can be considered a well-balanced person. We all need to have all three ego states available for use if we are to be well-adapted to life's demands. A completely balanced person has his energy evenly distributed between his three ego states, so that his whole self can be represented by three circles of equal size, surrounded by his skin, as below.

Such perfect balance of ego states is just as rare in real life as the totally *un*balanced types described earlier. And it would probably be a pretty dull world if we all were so balanced. We need people with a little extra Parent to be our good doctors and nurses and counsellors and ministers of religion. We need people with a little extra Adult to be our good lawyers and scientists and research workers and computer operators. And we need people with a little extra Child to be our good artists and entertainers and inventors and dress designers.

The vast majority of us, fortunately, have a good blend of all three ego states – enough of each to make us able to respond appropriately to most situations, but with enough preponderance of one ego state to make us especially adept in some particular area of life. The diagrams below represent the six possible ways in which energy may be unevenly distributed amongst the ego states within a whole person. (For the sake of completion, the perfectionist reader may like to add the instances of two ego states having equal amounts of energy and the third more or less energy, as well as the idealized version of the personality in which energy is evenly distributed amongst all three ego states.) Which type are you?

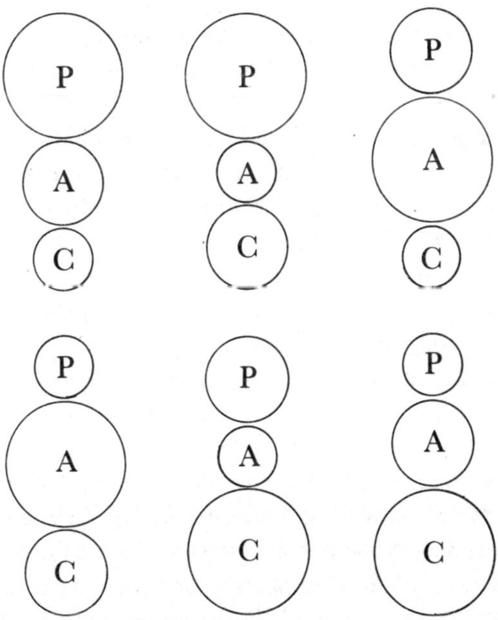

WHAT KIND OF STROKES?

We give a stroke to another person every time we do or say anything that acknowledges his presence. Any intentional body contact made with another person is a stroke, but so, too, are words and many other symbols that show that we are aware of the other person. Thus a smile, a frown, a telephone call, an invitation, a thank-you note, or a threat are all received as strokes, as well as pats on the arm, smacks, kisses or kicks. Strokes vary in their intensity and value from the most highly prized 'I love you' to the very slightly valued nod of recognition from a passing acquaintance.

Strokes can be given from and received by any of our ego states. Since each person has three ego states there are nine different ways in which one person can give another a stroke. However, some kinds of strokes are much more common than others. In practice, most strokes are Adult to Adult, Child to Parent, Parent to Child, or Child to Child, since transactions of either the Parent or Child with the Adult tend to be confined to the special teacher-pupil relationship, while Parent to Parent transactions tend to be confined to the relationship between a mother and father (or other authority figures) when they are specifically considering their children (or other 'subordinates').

In everyday life, our reactions to other people are based at least as much on *how* they say what they say as on the literal content of the transaction. This is easy to demonstrate with many simple remarks such as: 'What's for supper?', which the reader will readily see may be uttered from any of the three ego states of one person and be addressed to any of the three ego states of another person. So much of the meaning of everything we say to each other is contained in our tones of voice, inflexions and accompanying body language.

So, with only the stimulus of printed words on a page, it is difficult to define the nature of a transaction unambiguously. Nevertheless, for the record, let us consider each of the nine ways that one person can give another a stroke. See if you can work out for yourself which ego state is probably giving the stroke and which ego state in the other person is probably receiving the stroke in the examples below. (The answers are at the end of this chapter.)

1. Stranger to stranger in the street: 'Excuse me, could you tell me the time?'
2. Boy to girl: 'You're the most beautiful girl I've ever met.'
3. Husband to wife: 'We must get a kid-proof lock on this bathroom cabinet.'
4. Pupil to teacher: 'What should I do next?'
5. Ten-year-old to his parents: 'You stay in bed and I'll make breakfast.
6. Mother to whining three-year-old on the bus: 'Don't cry, we'll soon be home and then you can have some lunch and a nice rest.'
7. Father to son: 'You'll never saw a straight piece of wood that way. Here, let me show you how.'
8. Girl to boy: 'You are clever.'
9. Woman to man: 'Will you buy me a diamond engagement ring?'

Positive and negative strokes. So far we have only considered strokes that, to a greater or lesser extent, make us *feel good.* Granted, it probably doesn't do us a power of good to be asked the time by a stranger in the street, but at least we've been allowed to feel useful to another human being, even though just for a moment. Strokes that make us feel good are called *positive strokes.* But our need for strokes is so great that any stroke is better than none. We would rather receive a *negative stroke* – that is, an angry word, a put-down or a hostile glance – than be *ignored*, that is receive no stroke at all. Every parent and teacher is familiar with the child who, being unable to get any positive strokes for being 'good', at least makes sure of getting some negative strokes for being 'bad'. And even though grown-ups may be more subtle about it than children, we are actually no different. How often have you said – or heard somebody else say: '(S)he's always the centre of attention?' (that is, always getting strokes). Depending on whether the person thus noticed seems to give and get mostly positive or mostly negative strokes, we tend to envy and admire them or to dislike and criticize them for so doing. When we express admiration, we are giving positive strokes; when we criticize, we are giving negative strokes.

It is a sad irony that emotionally as well as economically the rich tend to get richer and the poor to get poorer. Receiving positive strokes induces the recipient to give positive strokes which, in turn, encourages others to give him more positive strokes. . . . Unfortunately, exactly the same applies to negative strokes. The nastiest people are almost always those who feel nastiest towards themselves as well as others. Breaking into the vicious cycle of negative strokes – usually begun in childhood – is a very difficult task, and probably the chief task of all kinds of psychotherapy.

Target Strokes. For each individual, some strokes are more valuable than others. The strokes we value most are called our *target strokes.* We each have positive and negative target strokes, respectively the things we like most and like least about ourselves. When we are given our positive target stroke(s) we feel great pleasure, when we are given our negative target stroke(s) we feel great pain. As in the case of each person's more general propensity to invite positive or negative strokes, each person's target strokes, too, are usually conditioned in childhood. Some common positive target strokes are for looks, intelligence, generosity and sympathy; some common negative target strokes are for stupidity, selfishness, meanness and untrustworthiness.

The target strokes for a particular individual are often hard to discern without direct questioning, although a clue to them is what kind of strokes the person tends to give to others. Thus, 'What a kind woman' is likely to be said by a woman whose own (positive) target stroke is her kindness; 'What a mean bastard' is likely to be said by someone whose own (negative) target stroke is meanness.

We tend to assume that other people's target strokes are the same as ours, but in this we are often mistaken. But it's worth finding out what a friend's target strokes are, because there is nothing more conducive to good feeling between people than giving someone a stroke you know she particularly appreciates and scrupulously avoiding giving her those you know cause her particular pain. Many unhappy relationships revolve around each person continually giving the other negative target strokes.

In our society, where praising our own good attributes (that is, giving ourselves positive strokes) tends to be frowned on as 'not nice', many people are inhibited about admitting their positive target strokes – even to themselves. If you have difficulty putting your finger on your target strokes, ask yourself the following questions: For your positive target stroke(s): What do I like most about myself? What was (were) the nicest thing(s) my parents said about me when I was a child?

The answers to these two questions will probable coincide and will define your positive target strokes. Similarly, discover your negative target stroke(s) by asking yourself: What do I least like about myself? What was (were) the worst thing(s) my parents said about me when I was a child? The self-conscious avoidance of people who regularly give us our negative target strokes is one of the surest ways of increasing our overall social happiness.

WAYS OF LOOKING AT LIFE

The Objective Physical World. In our ways of looking at objective reality we are all very much alike. We differ from each other to the extent that we each have our own particular ways of perceiving that highlight some, and gloss over other, aspects of reality. Thus an artist may tend to see 'nothing but' colours and shapes, a banker will focus on the economic aspects of reality, and a naturalist may find city streets 'empty'. Nevertheless, allowing for the differences of focus that are conditioned by differences of interest, by and large we have all been taught to interpret the world in ways that all sane people call 'correct'.

Consider, for example, a conversation between a five-year-old and his or her mother.

Five-year-old: 'Mummy, why won't my ball stay up?'
Mother: 'Because everything falls back to the ground.'
Five-year-old: 'Why?'
Mother: 'Gravity makes everything fall down.'
OR
Five-year-old: 'Mummy, why are all the big aeroplanes at the airport and all the little aeroplanes in the sky?'
Mother: 'The ones in the sky are just as big as the ones at the airport. They just *look* little because they're a long way away.'

Almost certainly our five-year-old will immediately and happily accept her mother's answers to such questions. Each answer she is given to all such questions she asks about the nature of the world makes the world, for her, a more *predictable* place. She *knows* a bit more and feels that much more secure.

And so, step by step, we accumulate in our Adult ego states all the many thousands of bits of information about the world that we all share. After infancy it is not only our mothers and fathers who give us all this information. From the time we start school – at the latest – books and teachers and television and other children provide additional ways of satisfying our continuing quest to *know things.* Through the increasing diversity of our sources of information, the older we get the more different we become from each other in the totality of what we know. Our interests diverge, and we get to know about some things in very great depth and detail while being satisfied to know comparatively little about other things. But the most basic facts about the world – facts that are most important for us to know in order to feel secure in everyday life – are the same for all of us and were learnt at our mother's knee.

The Subjective Psychological World. In exactly the same way and in order to fulfil the same basic need to make sense of the world so as to feel *secure* in it, we learn about psychological reality. Learning about physical reality enables us safely and confidently to interact with *things*, learning about psychological reality enables us safely and confidently to interact with *people.* Making sense of people means learning *how to give and get strokes.*

All the time we are asking our mothers and fathers about gravity and temperature, animals and birds, night and day, sand and snow . . . and about a thousand and one other physical realities that impinge on us, we are also asking about men and women, life and death, love and hate, anger, jealousy, ownership rights and sharing, happiness and unhappiness, good and bad, reward and punishment, etc., etc. And so, by the time we first leave home to go to school, we are basically equipped to get our stroke needs met in the world at large.

However, we all make one huge mistake – a mistake that most people continue to make for the rest of their lives. *We presume that just because everybody else's physical reality is the same as our own, so everybody else's psychological reality is the same as our own. It isn't.*

True, there are large areas of overlap between one person's and another's psychological realities, or else we would all continually fail to get strokes from other people. But the truth – however uncomfortable – needs to be faced, namely that unhappy relationships arise because each person's stroke needs and learnt ways of getting his stroke needs met are to a large extent unique. What we witnessed and were told about people in our early family life may be very different from what our best friend witnessed and was told about in his family. Some families are generally amiable, some sad, some angry and quarrelsome, some loving, some rejecting, some quiet, some noisy, some organized, some chaotic, some changeable. But it is on the basis of the characteristics of our own particular family that each of us *decides what human nature and living are all about*, and carries these decisions with him for the rest of his life.

In this way one child becomes the man whose greatest happiness is his close and loving family life, his greatest difficulty in life being his constant worry about money. Another becomes renowned in his field of work and feels immensely rewarded by the honours heaped on him, but constantly does battle with his inclination to alcoholism. One woman is constantly appreciated for her femininity and beauty but feels inferior for never having completed her secondary schooling, while another is profoundly positively stroked as a mother but miserable as a wife.

Thus – for the good and the bad in our lives – what is *relevant* to one person is *irrelevant* to another. Wealth versus poverty, health versus illness, fame versus anonymity, faith versus doubt, intelligence versus stupidity, beauty versus ugliness, security versus adventure are some of the commoner dimensions to be found in people's psychological make-ups.

Discovering the dimensions that are relevant to a particular person is revealing the nature of that person at the profoundest level. We will now turn to a consideration of what enables us to discover our own *unique psychological reality* in order to match ourselves happily to the unique reality of another. The sense *you* make of the world in combination with the sense your mate makes of the world is the essence of compatibility – or incompatibility.

As a start, to illustrate this central truth that *we are not all the same in our stroke needs*, imagine the following situation: it is December 23rd and you bump into a friend who has sent you a Christmas card, but you have not sent one to him/her. How do you feel? (Answer spontaneously and briefly.) Your answer almost certainly represents one of your *target negative strokes*. Ask the same question of a few of your friends and acquaintances. You'll be amazed at the variety of their responses.

Answers to quiz. 1. Adult to Adult 2. Child to Child 3. Parent to Parent 4. Adult to Parent 5. Parent to Child 6. Adult to Child 7. Parent to Adult 8. Child to Adult 9. Child to Parent.

CHAPTER THREE

Our Believing Selves – Character

Our Parent ego state is formed out of the things we are taught by our parents about 'good' and 'bad' and 'right' and 'wrong'. Although it is basically formed in early childhood, our Parent ego state is capable of growth and change throughout our lives. It consists of our beliefs and values and ideas about life in general. Some of our Parent values are shared with nearly all other people in our society, while some of them are highly individual. Our Parent ego state protects, controls and cares for ourselves and others. Its greatest contribution to the 'whole self', once it is fully formed, is its automatic action which so enables us to act well without having to think.

HOW THE PARENT IS FORMED

Our Parent ego state is basically formed between the ages of three and six, but usually needs a little polishing up in adolescence before the child goes out into the world as an independent adult. Between the ages of three and six we are *taught* by our mothers and fathers to be honest, kind, truthful, helpful and generally to share with and care for other people. All these principles are taught to us by explicit verbal exhortation and are reinforced when we observe our mothers and fathers and other people influential in our lives practising what they preach. By the age of about six, we firmly *believe* in all these moral principles, and these principles constitute our *character*.

Before the age of about three we are not capable of truly considering other people, although very young children do sometimes *look* as though they are acting from their Parent ego state. Consider, for example, a two-year-old girl who 'helps Mummy sweep the floor' with her own small broom. She may sweep the floor for a couple of minutes, but even the slightest distraction will prompt her to drop her broom, walk right through the dirt she has swept, and be off. Or perhaps she has a bar of chocolate, which she 'parentally' shares with her doll, but, of course, ends up 'eating it for Dolly'.

Such ways of behaving on the part of a toddler are only *imitative* of Parent behaviour. In order for behaviour to qualify as truly Parental it must be based on *a general moral principle* – which a two-year-old is too young to be able to understand. But by the time our two-year-old has become five or six, she will be capable of *really* 'helping Mummy'. If a friend comes round to play while she is sweeping the floor for her mother, she may well say to her friend, 'I'm just doing this for Mummy, then I can come and play.' Similarly, she will be capable of *really* sharing a bar of chocolate with another person.

For all human beings – as well as for all other species of life – there are well-defined 'stages of development', which correspond to ages when it is most *natural* for some particular kind of learning to take place. And three to six is the natural time for children to acquire their Parent ego state. Because this is the natural time to acquire our Parent ego state, the values and principles that we are taught then are very powerfully incorporated into our 'whole self'. The Parent ego state is always *taught*; morality does not occur naturally to children. Children who are not taught the Golden Rule and other values at this critical stage – between the ages of about three and six – grow up deficient in the capacity appropriately to nurture and control both themselves and other people. In extreme cases, Parent ego state deficiency results, later, in the psychopathic personality. While it remains possible to acquire basic Parent values later on in life, practically speaking, it is probably never possible completely to make up for its basic neglect between the ages of three and six.

This however does not mean that we cannot enlarge our Parent ego state later. In fact, our Parent is capable of growth and change throughout our lives. Teachers, books and new people we meet may all offer us values we had not heard of before, and, if we like the sound of them, we can choose to expand our Parent with them.

WHAT THE PARENT CONTAINS

Our Parent ego state contains moral principles, values and ideas about *life in general*. As well as reflecting what each of our particular parents taught us, our Parent also reflects values that operate in society as a whole. In fact, there are probably a few Parent values that are common to all societies everywhere, such as that murder is wrong, as is sex between parents and their children or between brothers and sisters.

In our particular society, kindness, tolerance, achievement, honesty, truthfulness, reliability, generosity and good manners are examples of positive Parent values that most people are taught; and violence, brutality, meanness, dishonesty, laziness and bad manners are generally considered by most people's Parents to be negative character traits.

But for each of us there are also highly individual values – some taught us by our parents and some we make up for ourselves in adult life, based on the fruits of our own particular experiences.

Each family, as well as espousing various values that are shared by most people in the society of which the family is a part, usually have specific values of their own, often handed down from generation to generation. Some families, for example, are very keen on educational attainment, some value financial success, some value being of service to the community. Some families are religious, some intellectual, and some place great value on family life.

Families also vary in the value they place on the Parent ego state itself, which, in general terms, stands for duty, responsibility, discipline and delay of gratification in the interests of the future, and caring for others before oneself. These functions of the personality are often in direct conflict with the Child ego state, which generally seeks immediate gratification of its whims, irrespective of the future consequences or of others' needs. What any individual defines as the 'right' balance between Parent and Child in life in general is itself a Parent value.

What does *your* Parent contain? That is, what do you *believe in?* Begin by listing the beliefs and values you have that are common to most people in our society, then add those that were taught in your particular family, then those that you have picked up along the way from teachers and other people you may have admired and books you have read. Finally, add any values that you have made up for yourself – that is, generalizations from your own unique experiences.

By and large, the most distinguishing features of your character will be the values your parents taught you between the ages of three and six. But don't worry if you can't remember back that far. The things they told you later on are almost certainly more or less identical with what they told you then. But if you still have difficulty pinpointing the beliefs they communicated to you, ask yourself how each of them would be most likely to complete the sentence, 'The most important things to remember in life are . . .' (Some things will be about what you should *be*, others will be about what you should *do*).

WHAT THE PARENT DOES

Our Parent ego state *protects, controls and cares for* ourselves and other people. Most importantly, it tells our Child when to *stop* and when it's OK to *go*. Its greatest contribution to our 'whole self' is its *automatic action*. It is as if the rules of conduct our parents gave us so long ago, *concerning the right and good ways of looking after ourselves and others*, are stored in a tape in our heads and the tape is ready to be re-played instantly whenever the occasion calls for it.

Most of us don't have to think about what to do when we come across a crying, lost child; we *automatically* stop and comfort him and see if we can find his mother. We don't have to think about looking both ways before crossing the road, since our parents taught us the preciousness and vulnerability of our lives long ago; or about catching up with a stranger who inadvertently left his wallet in the shop where we both were; or about saying 'Good morning' in response to somebody saying 'Good morning' to us. These and many other everyday acts that are to do with looking after ourselves well and sharing with and caring for others are ways in which our Parent expresses itself. When we are acting from our Parent we feel comfortable and secure in our conviction that what we are doing is right and good.

It is our Parent that drops a ten pence piece into a charity box and bakes a cake for the church bazaar. It is our Parent that stops us having another drink before leaving a party to drive home. It is our Parent that signs a petition on behalf of a cause we believe in or is a member of a committee. It is our Parent that takes a Vitamin C tablet when we feel a cold coming on, and remembers to take an umbrella when it looks like rain. It is our Parent that reminds us to change our underwear and put on deodorant and wash our hands after going to the lavatory. It is our Parent that mows the lawn and cleans the oven and makes sure there's enough bread and milk in the house to last over the weekend. It is our Parent that turns down the Hi Fi before midnight so as not to disturb the neighbours, and arrives on time for appointments and keeps promises and pays our debts promptly.

What are the main areas in *your* life where you regularly use your Parent?

CHAPTER FOUR

Our Thinking Selves – Knowledge and Interests

As was indicated in Chapter 3, there are natural stages in human development, and for each stage there are some kinds of learning that can take place then with greater ease than at any other time. Most parents and teachers are instinctively aware of the special opportunities for particular kinds of learning that accompany each stage of child development and accordingly stress the development of one ego state rather than another at different ages.

For the Parent ego state, we have noted that the optimal time for its development is between the ages of three and six. The Adult ego state grows most naturally and easily between the ages of eighteen months to three years and from about six to twelve years.

Our Adult contains all the basic knowledge and skills everybody needs to manage well in a practical way in the grown-up world, as well as extra knowledge and interests that each person develops for him- or herself. Our Adult ego state thinks rather than feels, so its greatest contribution to the 'whole self' is its impartiality. It also enables us to enjoy being alone sometimes as well as adding to our pleasures in being with other people.

HOW THE ADULT IS FORMED

Our Adult ego state is formed out of *facts we learn.* Like our Parent, our Adult is capable of growth throughout our lives, but also has its own ages when its growth is most natural and therefore most rapid.

Our Adult ego state has its most natural and rapid development in two stages of our lives: first between the ages of about one and a half and three, when we are learning to *talk,* and later on between the ages of about six and twelve. The Adult ego state is clearly visible in a toddler by the time he is about eighteen months old.

The *facts* that our Adult ego state accumulates, basically provide us with the necessary *skills* for getting on in the world. Whereas our Parent ego state is basically concerned with our relationships to other people, our Adult ego state is concerned with our relationships to *things.* It is our Adult ego state that asks Why and What and When and How and Where and Who. And it is with our Adult that we learn how to blow our noses, how to build a tower of blocks, how to use the toilet, how to wash and dry our own hands, how to draw a picture, how to dress ourselves and tie our shoelaces, how to feed ourselves, how to make a sandcastle with a bucket and spade, and how to do a jigsaw puzzle. Until, by the time we go to nursery school, we are well equipped to spend at least short periods *entertaining ourselves.* That is, our Adult ego state enables us to *enjoy ourselves by ourselves,* without relying continuously on the presence of another human being. In this way our Adult provides us with ways of finding strokes from the inanimate world as well as from people.

When our Adult has acquired sufficient *information and practical skills* about the world, we are ready to leave our parents and *manage our lives* for ourselves. But the inanimate world is very complicated. It usually takes the first eighteen or twenty years of our lives for us to acquire the information and many skills we need to be capable of looking after ourselves effectively.

A large part of the task of forming our Adult ego state is handed over by parents to our teachers at school. Here – especially between the ages of about six and twelve – we rapidly acquire the most important skills for getting by in the world, *practically speaking.* We learn how to read and write and manipulate numbers, to tell the time, to cross the street safely, to use public transport, to use a map and a timetable and a telephone and money.

And alongside all these *necessary skills and objective knowledge* most of us are fortunate enough to be offered, as well, much more information and many other skills which broaden and deepen our *interests,* that is provide us with bonus ways of enjoying ourselves. We may learn to swim, play the piano, draw, ride a bike, roller skate, collect stamps, join the Scouts, go fishing, sailing, horseriding, play chess. All these activities, as well as such taken-for-granted daily activities of talking and watching television, continually add to the repertoire of our Adult in those most important years of primary school.

Later on, by way of finishing touches, before leaving our parents' home, we may learn how to drive a car and play bridge, have a bank account and learn to cook, write cheques and business letters and fill in forms. Until, by the age of eighteen or so, we are confident of being able to *manage the practical side of life for ourselves.*

Inevitably, in grown-up life, the environment continues to demand of us that we acquire new skills and knowledge in order to cope effectively with everyday living. Thus a 'good education' (in the narrowest sense, when only the development of the Adult ego state is considered) includes teaching the Adult how best to go about acquiring new knowledge and skills as and when the need arises.

WHAT THE ADULT CONTAINS

Our Adult ego state contains *information.* Much of the information accumulated in our Adults in the first twenty years of our lives is the same for all of us, since it is necessary for us to *know* so many things in order to manage our own lives in the grown-up world. But once the necessary basic information and skills are acquired, each person's Adult becomes more individual. We acquire our own special interests and skills.

In grown-up life it is usually in our ways of *earning a living* that our Adult finds its most obvious expression. Sometimes our jobs are the natural development out of an activity our Adult tried out in childhood, sometimes our Adult doesn't discover its own greatest interests until we are grown-up.

People whose Adults are really gratified in their ways of earning a living are very fortunate, since, apart from having a mate to love and be loved by, spending our working lives in ways that really *interest* us is probably the most important factor that determines our overall happiness.

People who, for one reason and another, are compelled to earn their livings in ways which do not gratify their Adults – that is in ways that do not interest them – often find compensation in *hobbies,* which for some people, are pursued for a lifetime and provide enormous gratification to the Adult.

What special interests does *your* Adult contain? And in which areas of *your* life does your Adult find its greatest satisfactions?

WHAT THE ADULT DOES

Our Adult ego state is our *computer*. It collects, stores, organizes and analyzes information. Its most important contribution to the 'whole self' is its *impartiality*. Its roles are *clear thinking and knowing how*, so it is a marvellous arbitrator in conflicts that occur within ourselves between our own Parent and Child ego states or between other people when they are fighting or arguing with each other. It is capable of mediation between Parent and Child, between Child and Child, and between Parent and Parent.

It is our Adult that can solve the problem of our Child wanting to buy an expensive dress that our Parent says is an unjustifiable extravagance, by persuading the Parent to indulge the Child if the Child is willing to do some overtime for its pleasure.

It is our Adult that says, *impartially*, to two children squabbling over a piece of cake, 'Now calm down and let's work this out sensibly,' and then finds, through its *know-how*, the solution of cutting the cake into two exactly equal pieces.

And it is our Adult that has the best chance of breaking up a row between an abortionist and an anti-abortionist by pointing out that their argument is based on differing assumptions and values, about which they will most sensibly agree to disagree.

It is our Adult that *knows* the trick of peeling onions without crying, that can touch type, and knows enough French to get by on a holiday in France. It is our Adult that budgets our income and expenditure, mends fuses, plans menus, writes shopping lists, reads car manuals and recipes and instructions for filling in a form. It is our Adult that organizes a neighbourhood street festival and measures windows for curtains and floors for carpets.

As well as providing us with all the know-how we need to manage our everyday lives efficiently and well, our Adult also provides us with many additional pleasures. Although the Adult itself does not feel, the knowledge and skills it has enables us to extend the ways in which we can get strokes for our feeling ego states, that is for our Parent and Child. The more Adult skills and interests we have the more able we are to enjoy ourselves by ourselves, that is the less dependent we become on other people to provide us with all our strokes. Although very few of us can manage for more than a few hours at a time without *some* strokes from other people – even if it's only a natter to the woman who runs the corner shop – our Adult enables us positively to enjoy being alone sometimes, rather than inevitably feeling desperately stroke-deprived whenever we are alone. Think of all the hobbies and interests that enable people to spend time happily alone – reading, gardening, sewing, car-tinkering, painting, photography, stamp-collecting, making or listening to music, swimming, horseriding.

What solitary activities does *your* Adult enable *you* to enjoy?

And, of course, as well as all the solitary pleasures our Adult offers us, it also often contributes greatly to the pleasures we derive from being with other people. Think of all the ways of enjoying being with other people that depend on our having appropriate Adult knowledge of skills – tennis, football, cricket, squash, debating, playing bridge, chess, poker, and all the 'shop talk' of people who have similar jobs. There is nothing duller than being cornered by someone who insistently bombards us with information *his* Adult finds fascinating but which is of no interest to us; but there is great and continuing pleasure in the Adult to Adult transactions of like minds.

What activities with other people does *your* Adult enable *you* to enjoy?

CHAPTER FIVE

Our Feeling Selves – Personality

Our Child ego state is what we are born with. It is our biological self, which is instinctual, and contains our most basic needs for food, drink, strokes, and making sense of the world. At first, our Child is only capable of distinguishing between overall satisfaction and overall pain, but gradually these are differentiated into a wide variety of pleasures and pains. Our Child behaviours which get positively stroked by our parents predispose us to experience life pleasurably; our Child behaviours which get negatively stroked by our parents predispose us to experience life painfully. Some negative strokes to our Child are necessary to constrain us from hurting ourselves or other people, but some only serve the purpose of our parents handing on to us their hang-ups. Understanding our own hang-ups is essential if we are to choose a mate who gives us more of our positive than our negative target strokes.

WHAT THE CHILD IS

Our Child ego state is what we are born with. The 'whole self' of a new-born baby looks like this.

We don't have to learn anything for our Child ego state to express itself; it is *instinctual.* It is our biological self, which contains our most basic needs for food, drink, strokes, and making sense of the world. Our Child also contains instinctive responses to the satisfactions or deprivations of these basic needs – gurgling as expression of satisfaction and screaming as expression of deprivation.

If our basic Child needs are not met, we die. Without either an Adult or a Parent ego state we are not equipped to meet our basic needs for ourselves. As new-born babies we are wholly dependent on the Parent and Adult ego states of *other people* for our survival. Only very slowly do we acquire the capacities needed to ensure our own survival.

A very few instances have been recorded of children between the ages of three and six, abandoned in the wild, who have survived, but generally speaking it takes many more years for our Parent and Adult to be sufficiently developed to take care of our needs even for short periods. The Parent ego state of our society expresses this knowledge in English law, which makes it illegal to leave a child *under the age of thirteen* alone in a house at night.

At first, the only food and drink we want is our *mother's*

milk; the only strokes we want are the physical ones that remove our *bodily pains*, such as the pains of indigestion, an open nappy pin or too tight clothing; and the only sense we make of the world is expressed in our instinctual *fears of loud noises and of our bodies lacking support – that is being dropped.*

Gradually, however, our Child ego state develops of its own accord. The original basic pleasure and pain of the new-born baby become differentiated into a very wide variety of pleasures and pains. Within only a few months, we begin to enjoy cereals and meat and fish and fruit and vegetables and orange juice and ice cream as well as milk. We begin to feel anger, rage, frustration, jealousy, greed and disappointment instead of just simple overall unhappiness; and we begin to express our pains with sulking, whining, stamping, banging and biting as well as just simple screaming. We begin to experience humour, surprise, affection, delight, joy, the pleasures of exploration and movement as well as simple overall satisfaction; and we begin to express our pleasures in smiling, laughing, jumping, cuddling, kissing, squealing and babbling as well as just simple gurgling or contented sleep.

Until, by the time we are about three years old – with the exception of our sexuality, which is not capable of its full expression for about another ten years – our repertoire of feeling is complete. *The totality of the feelings and expressiveness in our Child ego state is our personality.*

But we have not yet accounted for the fact that people's personalities are different from each other. We have indicated that the Child develops of its own accord and that the wide variety of feelings and desires contained in the developed Child ego state are common to us all. True, but why are some people's personalities basically sad, some exuberant, some bad-tempered, some sweet, some nervous, some placid, some mean, some generous, some especially musical, some very inventive, some particularly artistic? How is it that some of us 'live to eat', while others 'eat to live', some of us love shopping and bargain-hunting while others hate it? How come that some people are warm and outgoing and some cold and aloof, some self-confident and some self-deprecating, some open and some secretive, some serious and some jovial?

HOW THE CHILD GROWS – THE FREE AND THE ADAPTED CHILD

Although there is no doubt that each new-born baby exhibits an innate temperament that predisposes him to express himself emotionally in some ways more often than in others, all normal human beings are also innately capable of expressing the full range of human emotions. The evidence is overwhelming that our grown-up personalities are principally determined by the kind and quality of strokes we regularly received when very young – mostly *before the age of three.* These strokes – some positive and some negative – will determine *our own particular pleasures and pains for the rest of our lives.* Some of these pleasures and pains are not instinctive but learned.

The Child ego state that we are born with is called the *Free Child.* At birth, the whole of our personalities and, indeed, all the energy of our whole 'selves' is contained in it. Not until the age of about eighteen months is the Adult seen as a clear and separately functioning ego state, and the independently functioning Parent ego state is not established before about six years of age.

But long before the emergence of the Adult and the Parent – at the latest by about nine months, when a baby becomes mobile – *constraints* on the free expression of the Child become necessary. In the second half of the first year of life, babies learn such facts as that power-points and the stove and glass ornaments are taboo objects in their exploration of the world, that their screams will sometimes be ignored or given negative strokes and that some kinds of natural behaviour, such as smiling, can also be used manipulatively to get what they want.

This early learning consists of *conditioned responses* – responses conditioned by the strokes from our parents' and other caretakers' Child ego states. The positive strokes our Child receives form our *permissions*; the negative strokes our Child receives form our repertoire of *constraints* on our Free Child expressiveness. These constraints combine to form a new ego state, a sub-division of the Child called the *Adapted Child*. By the time a baby is one year old his personality looks like this.

The strokes that enable each of our ego states to grow and develop fully are given from the corresponding ego states in our parents. Although in a general way all parental behaviour may be interpreted as being overseen and supervised by the Parent ego states of mothers and fathers, in practice our Parent ego state is stroked by explicit exhortation from Mother's and Father's Parents, our Adult ego state is stroked by explanations from their Adults, and our Child ego state is stroked by physical contact and by expressions of emotion, which are mostly non-verbal.

THE NATURE OF THE FREE CHILD – PERMISSIONS

The feelings and expressiveness in our Child ego state that are instinctive are called our *Free Child*.

The Free Child is recognizable by its *spontaneity* and the fact that everybody else can immediately see that the feeling expressed is *appropriate* to the situation. We smile or laugh with Free Child amusement at a Marx Brothers film or a circus clown; we run with Free Child terror from a bull that is chasing us; we squeal with Free Child excitement on the Big Dipper; we smile with Free Child joy on meeting someone we like or love; we cry with Free Child grief at the death of someone we love; we shout with Free Child anger at someone who has hurt us; we lick our lips with Free Child satisfaction while eating an enjoyable meal; we wrinkle our noses in Free Child revulsion to a nasty smell.

All such Free Child feelings and expressions of feelings are natural to everybody. Yet each of us has our own particular set of Free Child pleasures and pains we are prone to express more often than others. *The Free Child pleasures and pains we are most prone to express are called our permissions. They are Free Child behaviours in us which were positively stroked by our parents – from Free Child to Free Child.*

The kinds of behaviour that are felt as positive strokes to our Free Child and thus form our *permissions* are few. Cuddling, kissing, smiling, laughing and physical play are the essential positive strokes our Child is capable of receiving. The more often and regularly our Child behaviours receive these strokes in early life, especially in our first three years or so, the more permissions we acquire – that is the greater becomes our repertoire of emotional expressiveness and the more frequently, throughout our lives, will we experience life as joyful.

As well as experiencing joyful emotions, the Free Child also experiences unhappiness and grief as natural responses to pain and loss. These emotions, too, are healthily made into permissions by appropriate stroking.

All normal parents naturally want their children to

experience joyous emotions often and painful emotions as rarely as possible. So most parents attempt something of a tightrope act with respect to sad and bad feelings, giving permission for their expression with appropriate sympathetic strokes, while, at the same time, not prolonging such stroking to the point where the child is encouraged to experience his unhappy feelings as most stroke-worthy.

As well as from the Free Child strokes our parents give us for our own Free Child behaviours, our permissions are also developed by our observations of our parents in their Free Childs, responding to other things. In seeing our parents in their Free Child ego states while engaged in some particular activity, we come to associate that activity with emotional expressiveness, which is its own reward. *Simply being allowed a particular expression of the Free Child is a stroke to that emotion or impulse in the Free Child.* When we observed one of our parents having a contented look on his or her face and looking generally relaxed while listening to music or reading a book we were being given permission to enjoy music and reading. When we observed Father talking animatedly about his work we were being given permission to enjoy work. When we observed Mother smiling and humming while she sewed or cooked we were being given permission to enjoy sewing and cooking. When we observed Father giving Mother a kiss and a cuddle and a pinch on the bottom we were being given permission to express affection and be sexy. When we saw Mother's face all screwed up in pain and heard her curse when she stubbed her toe, we were given permission to express pain and anger. And when we saw Father crying when Grandpa died, we were given permission to express grief.

All such Free Child behaviours on the part of our parents were experienced by us when we were growing up as positive strokes to the corresponding parts of our own Free Child.

And, because getting strokes is our chief motivation in life, *any strokes given to any part of us act as encouragement for us to express that part of ourselves more often.* It is the most important part of the way we make sense of the world to say to ourselves, 'Oh, I see, *that* behaviour gets strokes, I must do that more often.' So the greater the number and kind of explicit Free Child to Free Child strokes we were given, and the greater the number and kind of implicit ones we were given (in simply being allowed to express our natural impulses) the more often are we likely to be in our Free Child ego state for the rest of our lives.

What *permissions* were *you* given? That is, what Free Child behaviours and expressiveness were permitted in *your* family when you were growing up? Ask yourself in particular what you remember your mother and father *enjoying* – separately or with each other or with you.

The more permissions we have the better equipped we are to experience life fully and richly. But if it seems you were given only few permissions, don't despair. It's still possible to pick up new permissions in grown-up life. If you are aware of particular permissions you lack and would like to develop, make friends with people who have those permissions. Allow their Free Child to communicate to your Free Child and catch their permissions from them as you would catch a cold.

THE NATURE OF THE ADAPTED CHILD – RESTRICTIONS

The Free Child is, for all of us, the most natural ego state to be in. It is our biological self without any overlays of civilization. Our Free Child wants what it wants – now – without any consideration of whether it is possible (Adult) to get what it wants and without any regard for other people's feelings (Parent).

For about the first year of life it is natural and appropriate for parents to gratify – as far as is humanly possible – all the needs and demands of their babies. Most parents realize that it is healthy and normal for a baby to be wholly Free Child and for its Free Child demands to be granted as quickly as possible. So mothers and fathers, for the first year of their baby's life, generally tend to put aside their own Child wants, and muster all their energy into their Parent and Adult ego states, in order to look after the more or less constant demands of the Free Child in their baby. But there are practical and psychological limits to parents' capacities to devote all their energy to gratifying their baby's Free Child demands.

Practically speaking, as the baby's Free Child impulses become more and more diverse, it is impossible to keep up with his demands. In the space of five minutes, a two year old may vociferously demand, 'Pink milk' (irrespective of the fact that there is no strawberry flavouring left in the cupboard), the right to climb onto a second floor window sill and poke a knitting needle into a power point (irrespective of the dangers), and to watch the Muppets on television (irrespective of the fact that the only programme on at the moment is The News).

Psychologically speaking, as a baby becomes more and more mobile, the totally selfish demands of its Free Child begin to outstrip its parents' willingness to sacrifice their own Child needs and wants. Most parents are unwilling to have the walls of their houses crayoned on, or their books torn, or their hair pulled hard, or the tablecloth pulled off the table from under their plates. So, from the age of about one year, in the interests of *safety and socialization,* it is necessary for the Free Child of a baby to be *constrained.* But the trouble is that at one year of age we have very little Adult and no Parent. By the time we are four or five our Adult ego state is sufficiently developed for us to understand – at least partly – the reasons for not climbing on window ledges or touching a hot stove or running onto the road. And by the time we are five or six our Parent ego state is sufficiently developed for us to allow our mothers to have a short, undisturbed rest, to respect other people's property and generally abide by the Golden Rule.

However, between the ages of about one and three, when constraints on our Free Child are more and more a daily necessity, the only way of achieving these constraints is by our mothers and fathers giving us *negative strokes* – which make us feel bad. Most commonly, these negative strokes take the form of a *smack or an angry look, accompanied by 'Don't'.*

'Don't touch the stove.' 'Don't pull the cat's tail.' 'Don't scream.' 'Don't pick your nose.' 'Don't touch my books.' 'Don't take that girl's doll.' 'Don't touch . . .' 'Don't take . . .' 'Don't hurt . . .' until, very quickly, the young child takes in these prohibitions so powerfully that he *automatically responds to them even when Mother or Father is not around.* If he disobeys a prohibition, he no longer needs Mother or Father to smack him or give him an angry look; *he gives himself a negative stroke in the form of a bad feeling.*

Once the child realizes that certain Free Child behaviours get negative strokes, he has two options with respect to these behaviours: *either he avoids the prohibited behaviour and so avoids the associated negative stroke, or he does what his Free Child wants and gets the negative stroke.* These two options are so powerfully incorporated into our Child between the ages of one and three that *they stay with us for the rest of our lives.* So for all grown-ups there is a whole range of Free Child behaviours which we *automatically forbid ourselves* or else, if we transgress the prohibition, *punish ourselves with a negative stroke – that is a bad feeling.*

For most people these restrictions include inhibition of such Free Child behaviours as nose-picking, farting or belching in public, aggressively demanding what we want, interrupting other people's conversations, kicking, spitting, or biting other people or animals, snatching things and sneezing or coughing in other people's faces. *The sum total of all such inhibitions in our Child is called our Adapted Child,* which is the constraining sub-division of the Child ego state. Because it is part of the Child ego state, it is part of our *feeling* selves. The Free Child and the Adapted Child together make up the whole Child ego state.

HOW THE ADAPTED CHILD CREATES HANG-UPS

So far so good. Few people would argue that the Adapted Child constraints so far mentioned are a bad thing. They serve the very important purposes of helping to prevent us hurting ourselves or other people long before we have sufficient Adult to understand the dangers in the world or sufficient Parent to take into account the needs and wishes of other people as well as of ourselves.

Later on, when our Adult is sufficiently developed, we will *understand the reasons for* such constraints as not running into the road; and when our Parent is sufficiently developed we will *believe in* sharing our chocolate with a friend. Theoretically, from the age of about six we are capable of *reasoned and compassionate judgements* about all circumstances as they arise. But in practice, at the age of six, we are still – and will be for many years to come – seriously handicapped in making right judgements because of the comparative paucity of our Adult knowledge about many everyday circumstances that grown-ups have learnt to handle with ease. For a long time yet we will need to go on learning many facts – like how to use a telephone directory, how to keep our money safe, and the risks of accepting offered lifts – before we are capable of functioning effectively and safely in the grown-up world.

Meanwhile, our Adapted Child ego state's implicit obedience to the rules imposed on it, our *automatic conditioned responses to physically dangerous or socially demanding situations*, keep us secure from multifarious physical and psychological hazards in our environment.

Our Parent ego state, as it grows, will come to contain many precepts consistent with the precepts in our Adapted Child ego state. Together, the Parent and the Adapted Child form a powerful alliance against the unrestrained expressiveness of the Free Child, and, normally, in childhood, the Adapted Child accepts its own rules and imposes them on the Free Child without question. Later on, in adolescence, it is part of natural development for the Adapted Child to do a flip and temporarily express itself as *rebelliousness rather than compliance*. Manifestly, the adolescent Adapted Child acts as if demanding total gratification for the Free Child and total disobedience of the Parent, but, in the normal course of events, maturity is achieved and is manifest as a restored equilibrium between all the ego states of the 'whole self'.

In grown-up life it is often difficult to distinguish between the Adapted Child and Parent ego states because the *rule-bound behaviours* they exhibit are so alike. The difference is that the Adapted Child is *specific and rigid*, whereas the true Parent acts from *general principles and is flexible*. If so conditioned, the Adapted Child may *never* eat chocolates after 7 p.m. (without feeling bad, that is), whereas the Parent, acting on the general principle that teeth should be cleaned after eating chocolate in order to avoid tooth decay, will allow the Child some chocolate in the evening, so long as the teeth are cleaned afterwards (even if they have also been cleaned just before). The Adapted Child may *never* tell a lie, (without feeling bad), but the Parent will understand the positive value of white lies sometimes. The Adapted Child will *never* allow the Free Child to play before the Parent's work is done, (without feeling bad), but the Parent is capable of making considered exceptions to this rule.

The Parent, like the Adapted Child, is basically rule-bound, but the Parent understands the meaning of the rules, whereas the Adapted Child does not.

As well as the generally unnecessary rigidity that our Adapted Child continues to impose on us long after such rigidity has outlived its usefulness, it also imposes constraints on us that were not even necessary in the first place. Along with all the constraints that our parents impose on our Free Child in the interests of our safety and sociability, they also impose *all sorts of restrictions on our Free Child that serve no useful purpose at all.* And since, between the ages of about one and three, when all these restrictions are imposed, we are in no position to discriminate between what is necessary and what is unnecessary, we all end up with at least some Free Child prohibitions that do us no good at all and only cause us pain.

The prohibitions that are imposed on us in the interests of our safety and our socialization are usually given by negative strokes that are a mixture of words and actions. Our parents are quite willing to say angrily and in public, 'Don't kick that cat,' or 'Don't scratch,' or 'Don't touch that,' and also are often willing publicly to accompany these words by a smack. In such instances, their Adapted Child joins forces with their (socially acceptable and respectable) Parent ego state. But the prohibitions that are imposed on us that are *unnecessary* – that is *the hang-ups in our parents that they pass on to us* – are communicated by their giving us *Adapted Child to Adapted Child negative strokes, which are often communicated without words at all.* And because these communications are often covert invitations to children to unhappiness of one kind or another, they are usually in direct contradiction to normal, respectable Parent messages, and are therefore usually given only in the privacy of intimate family life.

Since actions speak louder than words, these covertly conditioned Adapted Child responses will always have greater power in the child's life than the more explicitly given contradictory Parent values, no matter how vociferously the Parent messages are given. Adapted Child hang-ups get transmitted from generation to generation like a hot potato and 'the sins of the fathers are visited upon the children even unto the third and fourth generation.' (We will return to this matter in greater detail in Chapter 7.)

Thus a young child being pushed away when he tries to clamber onto his father's knee probably feels the injunction in his Adapted Child, 'Don't be close,' and is likely to have difficulty in forming intimate relationships when he is grown-up. An embarrassed look on the face of a mother whose child says, 'I hate my brother,' is probably received by the child as, 'Don't express bad feelings,' and she is likely to be rigidly polite and inauthentic in her emotional expressiveness for the rest of her life. An angry look given to a child who praises himself for something he has done well, is usually taken by the child to mean, 'Don't succeed,' and he is likely chronically to judge himself a failure, irrespective of his actual accomplishments. And a disgusted look given to a child who has accidentally soiled his pants, most likely means, 'Don't feel good about yourself,' and this child will grow up to be a perfectionist who chronically feels guilty about his own behaviour and is critically blemishing of other people as well.

How damaging to a child's overall happiness in life such messages turn out to be depends very much on how intensely and how frequently the messages were given in early childhood. Nevertheless, the commonplaceness of most of the messages just described ensures that few of us are free of unnecessarily repressive elements in our Adapted Child. *These useless, hurtful parts of our Adapted Child constitute our hang-ups and are basically responsible for all the unhappiness in our lives.*

Of all our ego states – Parent, Adult, Free Child and Adapted Child – the Adapted Child is the hardest one to discover in ourselves, for two reasons. First, because it contains our deepest pains, we naturally would prefer not to think about it, and so tend to run away from our awareness of it. Secondly, as has already been indicated, the Adapted Child often masquerades as Parent so that, for example, somebody who is overly polite because he or she has a prohibition against expressing anger may attempt to justify this Adapted Child hang-up with a Parent statement such as, 'Its inconsiderate to be angry with people.' Or somebody who has a prohibition against having fun may attempt to justify this hang-up with, 'The most important thing in life is to do your duty.'

Although there are very many possible Adapted Child prohibitions that may create hang-ups in us, they all tend to fall into five broad categories. These are:

Don't feel you are good enough (usually transmitted by highly moralistic, puritanical, perfectionist parents).

Don't ask for things for yourself (normally derived from environments where children are expected to be 'seen and not heard' and a 'stiff upper lip' is counted as the chief virtue).

Don't succeed (often transmitted by parents who have not achieved what they wanted and who bemoan their own lack of opportunity compared with all the opportunities they give their children).

Don't be yourself (usually given by class-conscious parents who worry about what the neighbours may think, and count propriety and good manners as prime virtues).

Don't feel you belong (usually transmitted by parents who act as if their children were a nuisance in their lives).

Nearly everybody experiences the pains of all five of these Adapted Child hang-ups on some occasions, but most of us have one or two which are a core part of our own Adapted Child and which we experience again and again in everyday life. Which of the five kinds of Adapted Child do you recognize as familiar parts of your own personality?

HOW OUR HANG-UPS ARE EXPRESSED

Our Adapted Child finds its expression in three roles we play – *Persecutor, Rescuer and Victim.* Eric Berne, the founder of TA, claimed that our impulses to play out these roles are so universal that they sum up all the characters ever found in all the fiction ever written, and account for the timeless appeal of fairy tales and myths, in which these roles are highlighted.

In our everyday transactions with other people, when we are in our Adapted Child ego state, we play out these roles compulsively, each player contributing to the ritualistic dance in which each player is unconsciously seeking to re-experience a familiar pain in his own Adapted Child. (Remember, negative strokes keep us alive as well as positive strokes, and the re-experiencing of our own familiar strokes which were conditioned in childhood also helps us to confirm our need to experience life as *predictable*.) Each of the players typically begins the dance in his own particular, favourite role, may flit around during the course of the dance amongst the other roles, but inevitably ends up in the role which is congruent with the Adapted Child hang-up he is unconsciously seeking to reinforce.

Unconsciously, we recognize at a glance the people who are willing and able to play the parts complementary to our own, and many intense but unhappy relationships are based on just this complementarity. Thus Mary (Victim), in a distraught state, rings Alison (Rescuer) to ask her advice and help in finding a flat. Alison (still Rescuer) comes up with various suggestions, 'Why don't you . . . ?', to all of which Mary (still Victim) responds with, 'Yes, but . . .' After some time, Alison realizes that Mary is not going to accept any of her suggestions, and flips into Persecutor, telling Mary, (still Victim) to do what she tells her or stop asking. Mary flips into Persecutor (the ultimate aim of the game for her), accuses Alison of not being a real friend, and slams the phone down. Alison flips into Victim (the ultimate aim of the game for her).

The precise Adapted Child feeling associated with each of the three roles varies amongst individuals according to the particular nature of their own Adapted Child hang-ups. But generally speaking, the Persecutor role has a feeling of *'Now I've got you, you son-of-a-bitch,'* the Rescuer role has a feeling of *self-righteousness*, and the Victim role has a feeling of *helplessness*. None of these ever feels really good to the person experiencing them, although they provide the comfort of familiarity when authentic positive strokes seem unobtainable. The preliminary moves leading up to the eventual payoff provide additional strokes as well as serving the purpose of hiding (from ourselves and others) the true nature of what we are doing, under the camouflage of socially acceptable transactions.

Don't-feel-you-are-good-enough people tend to begin as Persecutors (of others) and end up as Persecutors (of themselves).

Don't-ask-for-things-for-yourself people tend to start as Rescuers and end up as Victims.

Don't-succeed people tend to start as Persecutors and end up as Victims.

Don't-be-yourself people tend to start out as Victims and end up as Rescuers or Persecutors.

Don't-feel-you-belong people tend to start as Victims and end up as Persecutors.

Because our Adapted Child is responsible for most of the unhappiness we ever experience, *it is extemely important for us to recognize the core content of our own Adapted Child before choosing a mate.* Unless we come face to face with the realities of our own particular hang-ups, we will tend to choose a mate *unconsciously and impulsively, and that means choosing somebody who will tend to give us our own familiar negative target strokes at least as much as choosing somebody who will give us our own familiar positive target strokes. This is the central message of this book.*

Later on, in Chapters 7, 8 and 9, we will come back to the Adapted Child and will discover in more detail the part it plays in our lives. And in Chapters 10 and 11 take our own particular Adapted Child into account *in a positive way* in choosing a mate.

CHAPTER SIX

The Whole Self in Action

In the healthy 'whole person', the ego states are able to act collaboratively as well as independently. Parent and Adult collaborate to form judgements, Adult and Child collaborate to find alternatives, and Parent and Child collaborate to form compromises. Sometimes our ego states fail to collaborate, and impasses arise between them. Parent-Adult impasses are experienced as *indecisiveness*, such as, 'Shall I or shan't I buy this dress for myself? I've got enough money (Adult), but shouldn't I really save my money for something useful instead (Parent)?' Adult-Child impasses are experienced as *struggle*, such as, 'I want this dress so badly (Child), but then how will I find the money to pay the gas bill (Adult)?' Parent-Child impasses are experienced as *conflict*, such as, 'I want this dress so badly (Child), but if I buy it I'll feel terribly guilty for not being able to pay the gas bill promptly (Parent).'

When we fail to resolve impasses between ego states, we sometimes force the battling ego states into a truce, by providing them with a pseudo-solution that keeps both of them quiet. We achieve this by *contaminating* the impulses of the two warring egos with each other. Parent-Adult contaminations create *prejudice,* such as 'But this dress *is* useful;' Adult-Child contaminations create *delusion,* such as, 'I'm sure some money will turn up for the gas bill;' and Parent-Child contaminations create *confusion,* such as, 'Perhaps I can buy this dress and pay the gas bill with a post-dated cheque.' Contaminations may be broken up with the help of the third, uninvolved ego state, as we shall see.

HOW THE EGO STATES COLLABORATE EFFECTIVELY

A psychologically healthy, grown-up person has all her three ego states available at all times, and she is able to flip readily from one to another according to the needs of the situations she finds herself in. (For our present purpose it is not necessary to separate the Free Child and the Adapted Child. Together they are our *feeling self* which is all that is relevant to this chapter.) In her Parent when signing a petition for a cause she believes in, in her Adult when paying bills, and in her Child at a party, the healthy person feels and acts appropriately and so enables herself to be comfortable and confident in the world in general.

For many situations in life, however, one ego state is not sufficient to deal with an issue, and a well-integrated person is one in whom Parent, Adult and Child, as well as being able to act separately and independently of each other, can also be brought together to make joint decisions. The diagram below shows how *our three ego states collaborate within our 'whole self'*.

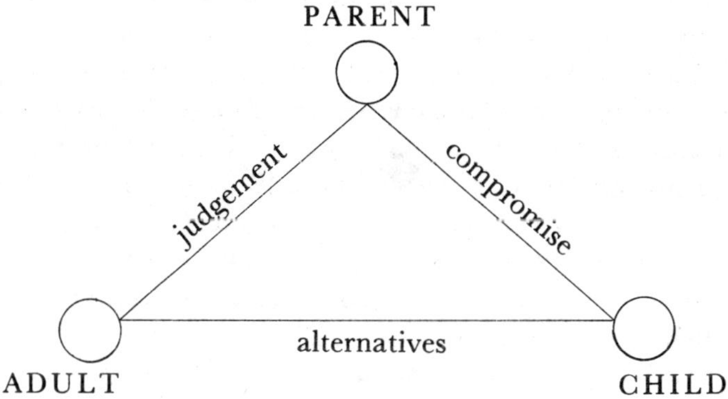

The Parent and Adult collaborate to form *judgements,* the Adult and Child find and choose between *alternatives,* and the Parent and Child form *compromises.*

Parent-Adult Collaboration. Consider the case of a judge in court, who combines the beliefs of his Parent with the knowledge of the law in his Adult before making a *judgement* and passing sentence. The Law itself is factual and therefore Adult. What is a crime and what is not a crime is usually unambiguously stated in the statute books, and a defendant is unambiguously found guilty or not found guilty.

Now in many countries the Parent values of society concerning crimes are also unambiguously stated in the statute books. That is, a particular crime is deemed to warrant a particular penalty, so in any particular case, once the defendant is found guilty, the judgement is pre-determined. In Britain this is not the case. Although maximum and minimum penalties for certain offences may be written into the statute books, there is usually very wide scope for the judge to bring his own Parent values to bear on the Adult reality of the law. And very often, in his summing up of a case, a judge will make quite clear what his Parent ego state believes, thus *justifying* the sentence he passes.

For example, in the case of a juvenile delinquent, before the court for the first time on a breaking and entering charge, perhaps the judge's Parent is harsh and says, 'Society should not have to tolerate such behaviour – ever. Two years.' Or perhaps his Parent is soft and says, 'Boys will be boys, but they grow up in the end. Don't do it again. Off you go.' The important point is that judgements vary, even when the Adult facts are unambiguous, because in all judgements the Parent ego state plays a part.

Think of a judgement *you* made recently. What were the Adult facts? Which of your Parent values or beliefs did you bring to bear on the situation? Do you have other Parent values that, if you had used them, would have altered your judgement?

Adult-Child Collaboration. Consider the case of a man who longs for a three-bedroomed house in the centre of town (Child). But the unpleasant fact (Adult) of its price – £50,000 – stands between his Child wish and its fulfilment. What might he do? He consults several building societies and his bank manager with his Adult, but comes away facing the Adult reality that, however he goes about it, his present salary and savings will only enable him to spend £30,000 on a roof over his head. So his Adult and Child collaborate and between them come up with a list of *alternatives:*

(1) a two-bedroomed flat in the centre of town.
(2) a three-bedroomed house in the suburbs
(3) save up and get a better-paid job until it is possible to buy a three-bedroomed house in the centre of town. Meanwhile, wait and buy nothing.

(4) move to a place where he could buy a three-bedroomed house in the centre of town for less money.

When our Adult and Child collaborate to discover various alternative ways of fulfilling our Child's wishes, we are being *creative*. And all creative acts consist of Adult-Child collaboration. A dressmaker cutting cloth to make it possible to get a dress out of it, a painter expressing herself within the constaints of her canvas, a housewife adding some water to the soup to make it stretch for an unexpected guest, a teacher 'drawing lots' with a class of children to select those who can have the six tickets he has been given for a pop concert, are all creatively bringing their Adults to bear on a situation where the Child cannot cope on its own.

In what ways have *your* Adult and Child collaborated recently? What did your Child want that it needed your Adult's help to get? How many *alternatives* did they come up with between them? Can you now think of any alternatives additional to the ones you came up with at the time?

Parent-Child Collaboration. Consider the case of a young woman who would like to exhibit her body as a night-club stripper (Child), but her Parent ego state says, 'What an immoral thing to want to do! Did I bring you up to be a prostitute?' (Once the Parent exhortations given us by our mothers and fathers in childhood – and often again in adolescence – are fully incorporated into our own Parent ego state we no longer need our parents to *enforce* our morality. No matter how far away from us they may actually be, we hear our mother's and father's voices in our own Parent ego state as loudly as if they were standing next to us.)

In this case, compared to the previous cases, the Adult is not involved. That is, there is *nothing factual* to prevent this girl from going right ahead and fulfilling her Child's exhibitionistic desire. But with a Parent ego state such as she has, she would be a fool to do so. *For ignoring its precepts, our Parent inevitably punishes us with inexorable guilt.* Were she to become a night-club stripper, the girl would discover all too quickly that her Child's pleasure was more than cancelled out by the pain of her guilty feelings invoked by the wrath of her Parent.

However all is not necessarily lost for her Child's wish. If she is aware that her primary wish is to exhibit her body, she may make a deal with her Parent. It may well be that her Parent does not particularly object to her exhibiting her body, but objects to the connotations of doing so in the context of being a night-club stripper. So this young girl asks her Parent's permission to be an artist's model and her Parent says, 'Fine, that's a very respectable profession,' and she becomes an artist's model and so gratifies her Child's wish to exhibit her body. Probably, being an artist's model is not *quite* so gratifying to her Child's wish as being a night-club stripper would have been, but the *compromise between Parent and Child* will have been very much worth it. Whatever pleasure her Child gets now – having obtained her Parent's permission – will be *without the pain of guilt.*

What compromises have *your* Parent and Child made recently? When did *your* Child last fly in the face of *your* Parent and get punished with guilt?

Parent-Adult-Child Collaboration. The most significant and far-reaching of life's decisions – such as marriage, divorce, to have or not to have children – require the harmony of all three ego states for a happy outcome to be achieved. This may account for the emphasis in traditional education – from the ancient Greeks to our present day – on the importance of games, since games usually provide an excellent medium for training the effective collaboration of all three ego states. Consider a boy playing football. His Parent is obeying the rules, his Adult skills are being exercised and developed, and his Child is having a marvellous time. His 'whole self' is represented by the point in the middle of the triangle in the diagram below.

A Boy Playing Football – The Whole Self in Harmony

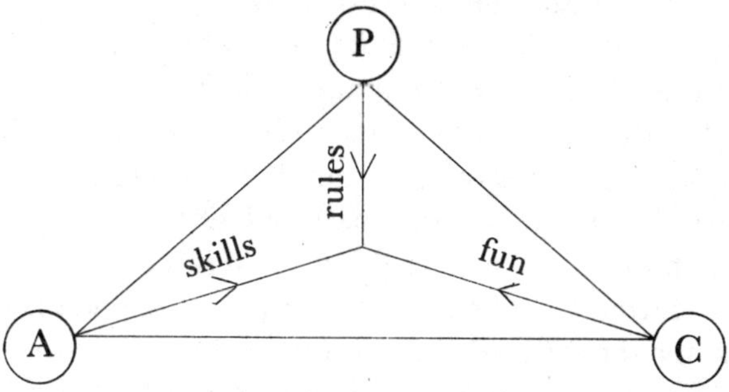

What do *you* do in everyday life that strokes all your ego states at the same time? What value in your Parent is stroked? What skills or information does your Adult bring to the situation? What is your Child expressing?

PROBLEMS OF THE SELF IN EVERYDAY LIFE

Unfortunately, however, life is not always as simple as we would like it to be. That is, our ego states are not always willing or able to co-operate with each other in the ways needed to solve our everyday problems easily. And, in all of us, there are some disagreements between our ego states that began when we were children, and which we continue to experience in Adult life as chronic difficulties in dealing with some kinds of issues in life.

Impasses Between Ego States. Consider the case of someone whose Parent contains very Socialist principles concerning the Welfare State, which include the view that nobody should be privileged, by dint of money, to buy an advantageous education for his children that others can't afford. Now the Adult facts are that the only state schools to which it is possible for him to send his children are notoriously badly equipped and understaffed and produce only a very small number of examination successes. What does he do?

His Parent and Adult talk it over. If his Parent principle wins, he sends his children to an available state school and hopes for the best. But perhaps his Adult argues that his Parent is being stupidly rigid, and that although, ideally, the state would provide an optimally advantageous education for all children, in fact it doesn't. Meanwhile, his Adult argues, it would not be immoral for him to spend his money on buying the education he wants for his children. If his Adult ego state wins, he consequently sends his children to a fee-paying school.

But if, in this debate, his Adult and his Parent are equally powerful and neither will give in, he becomes locked in an *impasse*. When the Parent and Adult are the ego states involved in the impasse, the experience of the 'whole self' is of *indecisiveness*. The person needs to make a *decision based on a judgement* but can't. If such indecisiveness about a particular issue continues unresolved, it may begin to dominate all his waking life and he feels chronically *anxious*.

Are there any Parent-Adult impasses in *your* life at the moment that are tending to make you feel anxious?

Adult-Child impasses are experienced as *struggle*. Consider the case of a woman married very unhappily to a brutal man who will not, however much his wife pleads, consider separation or divorce. This woman's Child longs to flee with her three young children, but the Adult reality of the situation is that she has no money of her own and no possibility she can see of earning enough money to support herself and her children and still be with them. Her Adult and Child struggle to find *alternatives* to resolve the impasse. Perhaps they come up with such ideas as:

(1) go to a women's refuge.
(2) wait till the children are all at school and then be free to get a job to support them.
(3) study or get some training which would enable her to earn a living later and would meanwhile distract hcr Child cgo statc from thc unhappiness of her marriage.
(4) put her children in Care and run away on her own.

If all the alternatives she comes up with either prove practically impossible (Adult) or go too much against her Child's wishes for her to carry them out, her Adult-Child impasse will turn from *struggle into chronic despair.*

Are there any Adult-Child impasses in *your* life at the moment that tend to make you despair?

Parent-Child impasses are experienced as *conflict.* Consider the case of an unhappily married man whose Child is in love with another woman, but whose Parent accepts his responsibilities to his marriage contract and towards the nurturing and rearing of his children. If, in the debate between his Parent and Child, his Parent wins, he stays married, gives up the other woman, and is unhappy. If his Child wins, he leaves his wife and children, but pays the price in his Parent of the loss of his children and suffers the *guilt* with which his Parent punishes his Child. If his Parent and Child have equal power in the argument between them, he may resolve the issue in the *compromise* of having a wife and mistress, but if the issue remains unresolved, his *conflict becomes chronic.*

Are there any Parent-Child impasses in *your* life that make you feel in conflict?

Contamination of Ego States. When we are experiencing *indecisiveness* between our Parent and Adult ego states, *struggle* between our Adult and Child ego states, or *conflict* between our Parent and Child ego states, we are working towards the respective resolutions of appropriate *judgement* (Parent-Adult) *alternatives* (Adult-Child), or *compromise* (Parent-Child). However unhappy an impasse between any two of our ego states may make us feel, we have every chance of eventually resolving their differences, because they are facing each other in *honest battle.* The resolution of an impasse may involve us in modifying our values or acknowledging realities we cannot change, or voluntarily curbing our desires, but every honest resolution will add to our competence in everyday living and may even make us wise.

There are however some impasses – either a new problem that crops up in our lives now or an old matter from childhood that continues to affect us – that are *too painful for us to face.* When we reach this point, we are inclined to cheat ourselves into feeling that there really is no problem. We force the battling ego states into a truce by providing them with *a pseudo-solution that keeps both of them quiet.* By this means *we feel better, but actually make things worse.* We achieve this by *contaminating* the relevant ego states, which is unnatural and an essentially *dishonest* thing to do, as we shall see.

Consider the case of a man whose Parent ego state was taught, 'All Black people are stupid.' (Some parents give their children some pretty nasty Parent values.) But Adult reality faces this man with a highly intelligent Black neighbour – a university professor of Philosophy – whose very great intelligence is an incontrovertible *fact.* Now the *honest* thing for our man to do would be to face the discomfort of the disagreement between his Adult and Parent and allow the perceived Adult reality of a very intelligent Black man to amend his Parent ego state. If he did this, he would be likely to form an appropriate judgement such as, 'I was brought up to believe all Black people are stupid. This is clearly not the case, so I no longer have this belief.' But renouncing our beliefs – even in the face of overwhelming facts – requires courage, and most people are more likely to attempt to bend the facts, if necessary, and cling tenaciously to their beliefs, however outdated. Our man with the Parent belief, 'All Black people are stupid,' is likely to decide, 'My Black neighbour is very intelligent, but of course he's the exception that proves the rule.' *This is prejudice.*

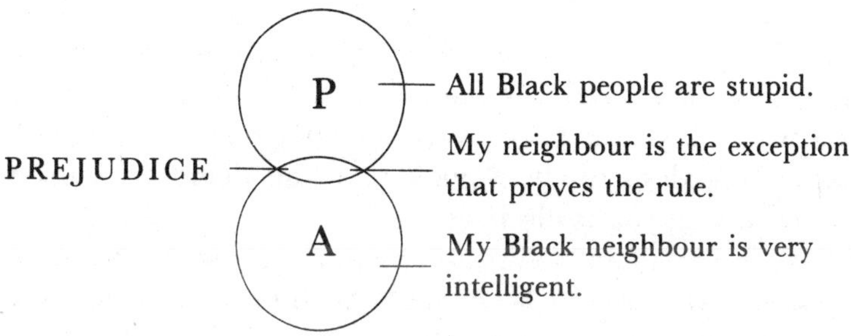

When people confront our *prejudices* we feel *threatened and anxious*. What *prejudices* are you aware of in people you know? Are you willing to admit to any prejudices of your own?

When the Adult and Child ego states are contaminated we have *delusion*. Consider the case of a girl whose Child ego state is in love with a man, but the man hardly knows her and certainly is not in love with her (Adult reality). The girl goes to a party where the man she loves is present. He doesn't talk to her all evening. If she cannot bear to face the reality that her feelings are not reciprocated, she may interpret the situation to suit her Child wishes and say to her best friend, the next day, 'He must be in love with me or he wouldn't have ignored me the way he did last night.'

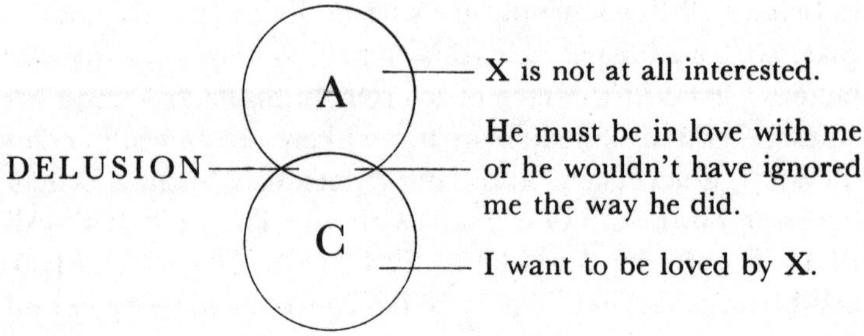

When our *delusions* are confronted we feel *desperate* in our impotence to get what we want. We feel like crying out, 'Stop the world, I want to get off! Can you remember ever wanting something desperately enough that you deluded yourself into thinking you could have it when, in fact, you couldn't?

When Parent and Child are contaminated we get *confusion.* Consider the case of a woman who tries on a dress in a department store. Her Child loves it and wants it but, to her Parent, to buy it would be grossly extravagant. She tries it on and takes it off several times, immobilized by her conflict, with neither ego state being willing to concede victory to the other. Finally, believing her Child to have won the battle, she writes out a cheque in payment for the dress and asks to have it sent to her home address. Three days later, the department store phones her and apologetically tells her that they cannot deliver the dress until she writes them another cheque, as she put next year's date on the original one.

Other people often perceive our confusions as *rigid inflexibility.* When we are confronted with our confusions we feel even more confused and are *unable to express our feelings clearly.* What Parent-Child disputes in *you* tend to confuse you? Can you state clearly what the disputes are about? That is, what

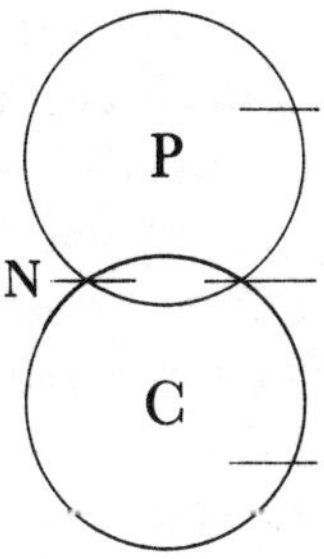

does your Parent believe that stands in the way of what your Child wants?

OVERCOMING PROBLEMS OF THE SELF

Choosing Honesty. By now it should be clear that *contaminations are pseudo-solutions to our problems* because they involve us in turning away from some aspect of reality. We form contaminations because facing and dealing with the realities we wish to evade would cause us pain and difficulty. But the man who made the prejudicial remark about his Black neighbour has not really justified his Parent belief; the girl who deluded herself that she was loved has not really achieved the love she wants; and the woman who wanted the dress is left hovering between having it and not having it. All of them have temporarily succeeded in *evading the pain of honestly facing the reality of their impasses.* The prejudiced man has not had to modify his cherished beliefs, the deluded girl has not had to face the pain of knowing she is unloved, and the woman in the dress shop has evaded the choice between self-denial and guilt. But their dishonest evasion of the truth has cost them dearly. Not only have they not got what *any* of their ego states wanted, but they have also *depleted the energy resources of the 'whole selves'*. The natural condition of our ego states is to be separate but in communication with each other. *Healthily*, the Child feels, the Adult thinks and the Parent believes; the Child and Adult collaborate to find creative alternatives to choose amongst, the Adult and Parent collaborate to form judgements, and the Parent and Child collaborate to make compromises. *Unhealthily*, the Child and Adult contaminate each other in delusion, the Parent and Adult contaminate each other in prejudice, and the Parent and Child contaminate each other in confusion. Contaminations are an unnatural condition for our ego states to be in. Contaminations are unstable and continue their precarious existences only so long as a large quantity of the energy resources of the 'whole self' is directed towards their maintenance.

Finding the Resolution. Unfortunately, because of the dishonesty with ourselves that is the essence of being in a contamination, it is very difficult to discern our own contaminations for ourselves. At the time we are in them, we inevitably believe in them. But it's usually quite easy to discern them in others. Ideally, the most productive way to break up our chronically incapacitating contaminations is to allow them to be confronted by others in a setting of mutual trust and love. In practice, it is rare for such effective confrontation to take place except in psychotherapy, since the Adapted Child vested interests of the confronter and the confronted almost inevitably hold sway on such issues.

In everyday transactions, the best way to break up our own or other people's contaminations, when we are aware of them, is to *bring in the third ego state, which is not involved in the contamination.* Thus the man expressing his prejudice about Black people may be more able to expose himself to the reality of the impasse between his Parent and Adult if approached by a *Child* ego state that says something like,

'How would *you feel* if someone said something like that about you?' The girl in love may be helped to break up her Adult-Child contamination by a *Parent* remark such as, 'Why bother with him? There are plenty more fish in the sea.' And the woman in the dress shop could be helped by an *Adult* ego state that proposed, 'If you can actually afford it, there's no reason why you shouldn't have it.'

When the contamination is broken up, the relevant ego states will be able to face each other honestly and achieve the collaboration that the 'whole self' so much wants, although the eventual collaboration depends on the individual's willingness to experience the necessary discomfort and to put in the necessary effort to resolve the impasse. When we are willing temporarily to experience *indecisiveness*, our Parent and Adult can resolve their differences into an effective *judgement* instead of anxiety or prejudice; when we are willing temporarily to experience *struggle*, our Adult and Child can resolve their differences into a choice of *alternatives* instead of despair or delusion; and when we are willing temporarily to experience *conflict*, our Parent and Child can resolve their differences into *compromise* instead of rigidity or confusion.

CHAPTER SEVEN

Childhood – The Crux of the Matter

We have so far discovered several different elements that go to make up our 'whole selves' – Parent, Adult and Child (Free and Adapted parts), positive and negative target strokes. We need to know all these elements in order to be able to choose a mate for compatibility rather than incompatibility. All the different elements can be put together in a single diagram to give us a composite picture of our 'whole selves'. Throughout our lives we seek a mixture of pleasure and pain, although our knowledge that we set things up to feel pain may be suppressed out of conscious awareness. It is inevitable that we seek negative as well as positive strokes, because we were conditioned to do so by the painful as well as pleasurable experiences of our childhoods. In adult life, our habitually sought and experienced pains are our hang-ups.

Let's take stock of how far we have come and how far we have yet to go. So far we have discovered that many different elements make up our 'whole selves' and the 'whole selves' of the people we choose for mates, so we need to separate out all these elements in order to recognize *what is crucial* in choosing a mate for compatibility rather than incompatibility.

We have discovered that the 'whole self' of each of us is made up of Parent, Adult, Free Child and Adapted Child ego states and that each of these ego states in each of us is in some ways like everybody else's and in some ways unique. We have discovered that all of us want strokes above all else, but that each of us has our own particular kinds of strokes – called our target strokes – that we want most. We have discovered that we have positive target strokes – which make us feel good – and negative target strokes – which make us feel bad.

We have also discovered that, as well as our need for strokes, we all have a need to make sense of the physical world of things and of the psychological world of people. It has been established that in the basic sense we make of the physical world of things we are all alike, but in the sense we make of the psychological world of people, in many respects we are all very different from each other. All in all, we *are* the consequence of the experiences of our childhoods.

Soon the reader will be in a position to put together all his or her newly-acquired knowledge into a composite picture of his or her 'whole self,' but first, the matter of pleasure and pain needs some further clarification.

WE SEEK A MIXTURE OF PLEASURE AND PAIN

We have already several times touched on the matter of our seeking pain as well as pleasure, negative as well as positive strokes, in our lives. In Chapter 5 it was shown that often our Adapted Child constraints on our Free Child are later supported by positive values fed into our growing Parent ego states, but it was also shown that some of our Adapted Child constraints are in direct contradiction of our Parent values, and that these *unnecessary* constraints form our hang-ups. How do we come to acquire such contradictory messages from our parents?

Two separate factors contribute to the realities that our parents give us contradictory messages and that we all chronically seek negative as well as positive strokes. These are the *unavoidability of things sometimes going wrong in our childhoods and the fact that parents pass on their hang-ups to their children.*

Inevitably, in the process of growing up, things go wrong in our families. Parents quarrel, fathers lose jobs, mothers get ill, the household is disrupted by the presence of a widowed grandparent. Though some of us as children are witnesses to more unhappiness than others, none of us completely escapes difficulties in our family life when we are young.

Such occurrences disrupt the smooth flow of positive strokes between parents and children in even the happiest of families. But, as we learnt in Chapter 2, our need for strokes is so central to our well-being that we would rather receive negative strokes than no strokes at all, and it is through the experience of family unhappiness that most children learn to seek negative strokes when no positive strokes are on offer.

Let us take, for example, the case of a three-year-old who witnesses his parents quarrelling. The first time he experiences this situation he is frightened, but nobody seems to notice it. His fear is not stroked. So next time his parents quarrel, he seeks to get strokes by being angry with them, shouting at them to stop. This response, too, is ignored. The next time he acts sad and cries, and this time he is noticed. One of his parents shouts, 'Stop that snivelling! I've got enough to contend with without you being inconsiderate as well.' This may be the first time he has ever heard the word 'inconsiderate', and he probably has no idea what it actually means, but from then on this word and the bad feeling he experienced at that time will be permanently ingrained in his Adapted Child as one of his *target negative strokes*. And whenever – for the rest of his life – he is, for any reason, feeling deprived of strokes he will set things up, (probably unconsciously) so that somebody will give him or he will give himself an 'inconsiderate' negative stroke. 'Don't be considerate,' will become one of his Adapted Child messages and even though his awareness of this message may be submerged, his obedience to it is likely to be a major and lifelong source of unhappiness to him in his relationships.

When things went wrong in your family, what bad feeling were you made to feel most often? Was that feeling your answer to the question at the end of Chapter 2?

The second factor that contributes to the inevitability that we all seek our own particular pains as well as our own particular pleasures is that parents have hang-ups which they pass on to their children. All normal parents want the best for their children, and pass on to them Parent messages like, 'Be honest,' 'Succeed in life,' 'Be loving and kind to others.' But ever since our expulsion from the Garden of Eden, life has never lived up to its ideal version for any of us, and each generation transmits its own experienced pains to the generation that comes after it. It is as if we find some solace for our miseries if we are able to tell ourselves that our particular pains are necessary and universal. We tend to avoid people who lack our pains because they bring us uncomfortably close to awareness that much of our pain is, in fact, self-inflicted. And so – albeit largely unconsciously – parents do their best to make sure their children are no happier than they themselves are, while consciously affirming their wish for their children's total contentment.

At a deep level parents are often ashamed of transmitting their own Adapted Child hang-ups to their children and so, instinctively, tend to reserve such transactions for the privacy of intimate family life. Often their Adapted Child hang-ups are in direct contradiction to their Parent values, which contradiction is exhibited in such behaviours as a father vehemently espousing the value of sobriety to his children, (Parent to Parent) and yet coming home drunk every other night (Adapted Child to Adapted Child injunction amounting to, 'Don't be sober.') Or a mother may frequently espouse to her children, Parent to Parent, that marriage is the surest way to happiness and yet have frequent unhappy rows with her husband (an Adapted Child to Adapted Child injunction amounting to, 'Don't be happily married.')

Now *actions speak louder than words*, and when Parent and Adapted Child messages are in conflict in us, *in the end the Adapted Child wins.* Very often, especially in early adult life, we succeed in living in accordance with our Parent messages only and manage to kid ourselves that we have cast off the effects of our Adapted Child messages, or even that we have none. *This self-deception is the single greatest cause of unhappiness in general and unhappy marriages in particular.* If, for example, our Parent says, 'Be happily married,' and our Adapted Child says, 'Don't be happily married,' we will *consciously* choose to marry someone we believe we will be happy with, but *unconsciously* we will choose that very same person for his or her characteristics that our Adapted Child knows will, in the end, achieve *its* aim of unhappiness. *Only by having the courage to make our Adapted Child conscious can we gain the power to choose – with our Adult – overall pleasure rather than overall pain.*

PUTTING IT ALL TOGETHER

If you have answered all the questions that this book has asked you about yourself so far, you have already discovered a great deal about your individuality. You already know which of your ego states you tend to use most often and which you tend to use least often. You know a great deal about the *contents* of your Parent, Adult and Child ego states and the *uses* you make of each of them in your life. You know the *permissions* you have in your Free Child and the *inhibitions* you have in your adapted Child.

Let's put all this information together to form a composite picture of the messages contained in all your ego states. Most of us were fortunate enough to be brought up by two parents, so the messages that fed our growing Free Child, Adapted Child, Adult and Parent ego states had two main sources, Mother and Father, (although grandparents, teachers, older brothers and sisters and others may also have been significant in our early learning). Whereas ordinary communication is possible between any ego state of one person and any ego state of another person, it makes most sense to understand messages received by our growing ego states as coming exclusively from the corresponding ego states of our Mother and Father. Their Child ego states teach our Child ego states, their Adult ego states teach our Adult ego states, and their Parent ego states teach our Parent ego states. So the contents of each of our ego states is an amalgamation of what we learnt from the corresponding ego states of both Mother and Father. All that we learnt from our parents can be summarized in a diagram showing Mother and Father, on either side of ourselves, sending us messages from their Parent, Adult and Child to our Parent, Adult and Child, as below.

Such a diagram is useful in enabling us to see at a glance the core contents of all the ego states that go to make up the 'whole self', and is particularly useful in discerning important contradictions that may exist between received Parent and Adapted Child messages. In grown-up life these contradictions within the 'whole self' may make an individual perceive himself as his own worst enemy. That is, he may self-consciously strive to fulfil his Parent messages and yet be chronically sabotaged in this striving by his submerged, contradictory Adapted Child messages. As has already been stressed, unless the Adapted Child messages are brought into full conscious awareness, in the end they will always win over the contradictory Parent messages, no matter how vociferously and repeatedly the Parent messages were given.

HOW OUR EGO STATES ARE FORMED BY MESSAGES FROM OUR PARENTS

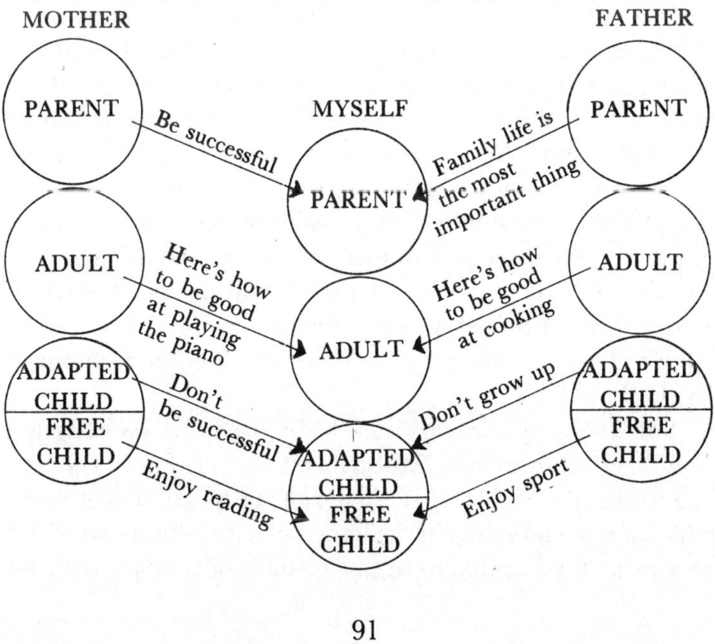

In the example above, just one message from each ego state of each parent has been given, but, of course, each of us actually gets at least several important messages from each ego state of each of our parents, as well as the very many messages we received in common with nearly everybody else, such as 'Stealing is wrong' (Parent), 'Here's how to read and write' (Adult), 'Don't snatch – ask politely' (Adapted Child) and 'Yum, yum' (Free Child permission to enjoy food). When you draw up your composite picture of *your* self, concentrate especially on the messages that were quite specific to your family – the Parent values *your* particular parents espoused most powerfully, the Adult skills they taught you, the positive strokes they gave your Free Child and the things they enjoyed themselves that gave you your permissions, and the negative strokes they gave your Free Child, which formed your Adapted Child.

Refer back to your answers to questions in Chapters 3, 4 and 5 in drawing up your composite picture of your own self. When in doubt as to where a particular message fits into the whole, remember that Parent messages are messages about what to *do* and *be* in a *positive way,* Adult messages are about *how to do* certain things well, Free Child messages are usually permissions to *enjoy* certain things. You may find it quite difficult to formulate your Adapted Child messages explicitly. If so, check your awareness of yourself against the five general categories of Adapted Child messages given in Chapter 5. Adapted Child messages always begin with 'Don't', because they are all restrictions on natural impulses in the Free Child.

The following diagram should be used for the messages you received from your Mother and Father. Fill in the messages along the lines of the diagram on p.93. (If you were unfortunate enough to be orphaned in early childhood or, for any reason, separated from one or both of your parents, for

'Mother' and 'Father' substitute the people who had most influence on your life when you were growing up.)

HOW YOUR EGO STATES WERE FORMED BY MESSAGES FROM YOUR PARENTS

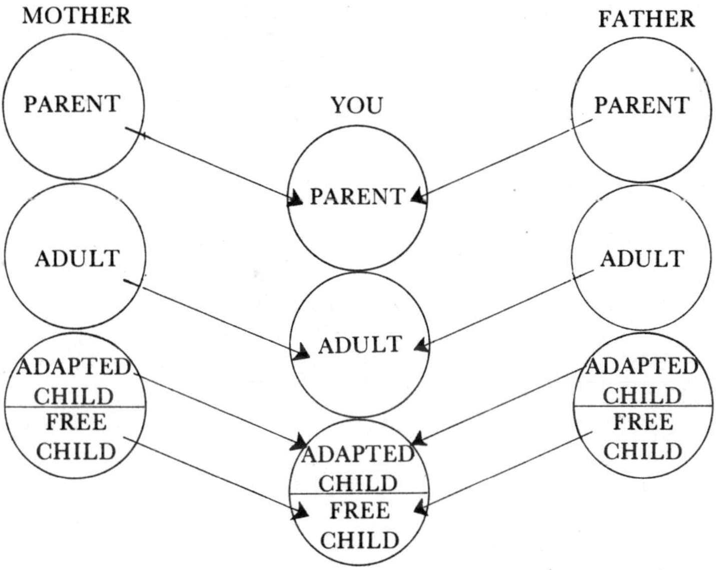

CHAPTER EIGHT

Decisions – the Core of Our Being

The messages our parents gave us taught us how to fulfil our need for strokes, but the messages in themselves are not sufficient to fulfil our other basic need, to make sense of the world. In the same way as we make sense of the physical world by learning generalizations about facts we experience, so we make sense of the psychological world by generalizing the meanings of the messages we received.

As has already been established in Chapters 1 and 2, there is no doubt that the sense each of us makes of the physical world is to some extent different from the sense any other person makes of the physical world, and the sense each of us makes of the psychological world is to some extent the same as the sense every other person makes of the psychological world. All of science depends on the continuous possibility of a given view of physical reality co-existing with or replacing a previous view; and all communication between people depends on the truth that there are important areas of overlap between one person's and another's perceptions of psychological reality. But, by and large, in everyday life, there is a huge amount of agreement between people concerning the nature of physical reality and – notwithstanding the widespread mistaken assumption to the contrary – there is comparatively very little agreement between people concerning the nature of psychological reality.

Generally speaking, parents and others tell us the 'correct' ways to make sense of the physical world, but we make sense of the psychological world for ourselves, making our own, sometimes unique, decisions about the meaning of our messages. Unconsciously, we all continually use our experience, throughout our lives, to confirm the decisions we originally made in childhood. By reference to important events we experienced in our childhood, it is possible to discover our decisions. Most decisions can be classified in terms of five types, and this chapter is concluded with a questionnaire which will facilitate your discovering the kinds of decisions prominent in your personality. This element of 'decisions' is the last component of our 'whole self' that needs to be revealed before the stage is set for us to choose a mate with all the Adult knowledge we need to make our choice a happy one.

MAKING SENSE OF OUR MESSAGES

The picture so far presented is of ourselves as children being *passive recipients* of the messages imposed on us by our parents, with no power to counteract their impositions, no matter how malefic we experience them to be. This is not the whole truth.

True, in early life, we do obey all the messages our parents gave us, because this obedience is the only way we can get strokes from them. And later on, when we no longer live with our parents, we are profoundly inclined to form relationships with other people who are willing and able to give us those same old strokes, because those were the ones we were taught to seek, and it doesn't occur to us that there may be others we could seek and find. But seeking and finding the strokes we were taught about in our early childhood fulfils only half of our most basic needs. *Our basic need to make sense of all the conglomeration of messages we received has not yet been accounted for.*

Remember back to Chapters 1 and 2, in which we outlined the kind of sense all sane people make of physical reality. 'Gravity makes everything thrown up *always* fall down,' 'Things at a distance *always* look smaller than they are,' 'Night *always* follows day.' The crucial ward is *'always'*, because only explanations that contain it provide us with the *predictability* that fulfils our inbuilt need to experience events in the world as *ordered rather than chaotic.* First we experience facts, then we put them together to *make a general truth.*

Now the *messages* our parents transmit from their ego states to our growing ego states are the *facts* of the psychological reality we experience. And, in the same way as for the physical facts, we make coherent sense of these psychological facts by making generalizations about them. These generalizations are our *decisions about life,* whose *fixed certainty* we need, and which we cherish with the same degree of conviction as that night always follows day or that balls thrown up always fall down.

True, even our most fixed and universally agreed certainties about physical reality are not absolutely invulnerable to any challenge, as the radical revolutions in science over the past five hundred years or so bear witness. But the visionary giants who eventually persuaded us of such things as that the earth goes round the sun rather than the other way round, that human beings have evolved, like all other species, rather than being eternally supreme on earth, and that children as well as grown-ups are sexual beings, had to be, as history makes clear, men of courage as well. Collectively, we fight tooth and claw, with denial, ridicule, inquisitions, and any other weapons we can muster, to defend the 'certainties' that provide us with our existential security.

Eventually, however, the ideas that started as threats to old 'certainties' themselves become new 'certainties', and we breathe a sigh of relief until a powerful enough new idea blows our minds open again. (It is my personal belief that much of the restlessness and anxiety for the future that seems so predominant a feature of human awareness in this century is a direct consequence of the newest cosmological 'certainty' that 'nothing is certain'. No wonder 'doomwatching' is so widespread.)

The above digression into metaphysics may seem a far cry from the promise of this book's title, but it is, in fact, very pertinent to our theme. With respect to the tenacity with which we cling to 'certainties', the analogy between the scientific knowledge of mankind and the psychological knowledge of individual human beings is perfect. For each of us, actually changing a profound psychological decision that was made in early childhood is, if at all possible, a very difficult task indeed. But, lest the reader be disheartened by this 'fatalism', later on in this chapter and again in Chapter 12, we will discover how even our rigid decisions contain loopholes of freedom. Meanwhile, we need to elucidate in more detail how we acquire and maintain the decisions that are the core or our being.

WE MAKE OUR OWN DECISIONS

Just as there are scientific truths that are sufficiently well-established that they are part of the 'commonsense' of all our lives, there are also, at a general level, some psychological truths that, in a given culture at a given time in history, tend to permeate the whole culture. Thus much of the 'revolutionary', 'incredible' teaching of Freud earlier this century has now sufficiently transformed our culture that Freud's once esoteric pronouncements are now understood by nearly everybody. Such concepts as the Oedipus complex and the pervasive importance of our earliest years of life are now taken to be 'obvious' to a very large proportion of educated people, and the films, plays and novels that imply the reality of these concepts are accepted and appreciated readily and immediately by their audiences.

So, implicitly, through the wide-ranging and pervasive media of culture, as well as through our parents, (who are, to us as children, to some extent spokesmen for the culture to which they belong,) we *are* given some broad generalizations about psychological reality. These generalizations form a comfortable background of similarity between ourselves and other people, even though we may remain unaware of their 'taught' nature unless and until we venture into another culture whose implicit assumptions are different enough from our own that we are 'misunderstood' at a level we never before dreamt was possible.

However, the psychological knowledge we share with all other members of our own culture, important as it is to our general comfort in society, is far from sufficient for our everyday needs in transacting with other people. In some isolated and primitive tribes, where individuality is scarcely evident, cultural generalizations may be all that really matters, but in our sophisticated, diversified culture, where the quest for individual 'self-realization' is held to be an innate right (and even a duty), a large part of 'my' psychological truth is very different from a large part of 'yours'. Whereas, with respect to the basic world of things, our parents, books and teachers accept most of the responsibility for informing us what generalizations are 'correct', in matters of psychology we are left to our own devices. *We make most of our decisions about psychological reality for ourselves.*

Even when our parents do offer us decisions – that is, generalizations about psychological reality that are their own rather than the culture's – along with their messages, there is almost always more than one way we can *choose* to use that decision in our life. For example, in one family the author knows well, the three children were all given the Adapted Child message, 'Don't fit into society.' They were all also saved the bother of making their own decisions about what *sense* to make of this message in their lives, by being offered – on a plate, as it were – the decision, 'You'll end up in court.' One of the three children became a drug addict, one became a thief and one became a lawyer.

As well as having to fit the 'facts' of our Adapted Child messages, our decisions also have to fit the 'facts' of our Parent, Adult and Free Child messages *at the same time*. So when we actually receive contradictory messages in our different ego states – as often is the case in our Parent and Adapted Child – making one decison to fit *all* relevant messages requires considerable cleverness. (We may even have contradictory messages *within* an ego state if, for example, Mother's Parent said , 'Always be gentle' and Father's Parent said, 'Be aggressive.') But our Adult ego state – even when only four or five years old – is nearly always capable of rising to the challenge, and somehow or other making a simple decision out of all the messages it has to cope with, however contradictory they may be. (In the rare cases where our Adult finds the task impossible, we have the seeds of madness.) *Our Adult makes the decisions, but the decisions themselves become part of our Adapted Child personality.*

Consider, for example, the case of a boy who receives the

following messages about sex from his father:
Parent message: 'Be sexy, be manly.'
Adult message: 'Here's how to dress smartly.'
Adapted Child message: 'Don't you dare compete with me sexually.'
Free Child message: 'Permission to enjoy male sports.'
Out of all this *the boy decides to be a homosexual sportsman.* His decision may remain forever unconscious, just as his decision, for example, that distant objects always look smaller than they are may remain essentially unconscious, but will nevertheless be fixed in him for life.

In grown-up life this boy becomes just what he decided – a champion footballer, say, with manly good looks and smart male clothes that make the teenage girls drool, but – unknown to the girls in love with him – a homosexual. It might well be that this boy has a mother who gave him an Adapted Child message, 'Don't leave me,' (since her sexy husband may well have neglected her for other women, and she turned to her son for strokes to her femininity.) If this is the case, the boy's decision to be homosexual is made even more powerful inasmuch as it satisfies his mother's Adapted Child message as well as his father's messages. That is, by being a homosexual he 'never leaves Mother for another woman' as well as not competing sexually with Father. (The recent increased *cultural* acceptability of homosexuality may have been to some extent influential in his decision. That is, society's *permission* to be homosexual may have simplified his task of making sense of his messages, whereas, at a time when society withheld this permission, he may have felt obliged to find a more difficult reconciliation of his messages.)

Powerful as are the messages our parents gave us about how to get strokes, *it is ultimately the decisions we made around them that rule our lives.*

We can, to some extent, once we have become aware of

them, choose *not* to obey some of our parents' messages. After all, they gave us plenty to choose from, so we can afford to forgo strokes from some messages and make up our stroke deficit by paying more attention to other messages. But to disavow a *decision* is radical surgery of the soul. A decision represents part of the sense we make of the world, so dropping it means giving up predictability in favour of chaos. Uri Geller may make us see things we have never seen before, and some of us are willing to believe that what he makes us see are *new facts* (rather than trickery), but how many of us are willing to infer from this that the laws of Physics are wrong? As has already been elucidated, the Laws of Physics, like our personal decisions about psychological reality, get changed only as a desperate last resort.

WE REPEATEDLY CONFIRM OUR DECISIONS

Just as we are instinctively compelled to obey the messages we received in order to fulfil our basic need for strokes, so we are instinctively compelled repetitively to 'prove' the 'correctness' of our decisions. But because we take our decisions so deeply for granted, they are to a large extent unconscious, so we may have some difficulty in accepting the fact that *we all set up our lives so that our experiences 'prove' our decisions over and over again.*

You may be helped to understand this by considering how we also repeatedly 'prove' our knowledge of the physical world – just for fun, as it were. Given a ball, how many of us can resist throwing it up – and experiencing the satisfaction that it fulfils our *prediction* that it will fall down because *it must?* Who has never kicked a stone along the pavement, or flicked a flat pebble over the surface of water, or made his voice echo in a cave, or covered a burning candle with a jar to watch it go out when the air is used up? In all such behaviours the satisfaction – however small that satisfaction may be – derives from the fact that the truth of something we know about the physical world is once again confirmed.

In exactly the same way, a very great deal of our behaviour with other people is, at least to some extent, unconsciously designed to confirm *our own individual truths contained in our decisions*. But a great deal of such behaviour is very subtle and difficult to discern for what it is. However, at least sometimes, we are aware of our compulsion to prove certain things over and over again. All of us occasionally say things like, 'Here I go again,' 'Why does this always happen to me?' '(S)he seems to invite accidents/misery/good luck/trouble.' All these statements are reflections of the truth that each of us does – in terms of our own particular decisions – repeat the same patterns of experience over and over again.

DISCOVERING YOUR DECISIONS

Because our decisions are to some extent unconscious they are difficult to discover for ourselves without the help of a skilled psychologist. However, just as in Chapter 5 we were able to generalize Adapted Child messages into five broad categories, so it can be shown that our decisions, too, can be generalized into five corresponding categories. We will discover the *types* of messages in your Adapted Child and the *types* of decisions you probably made in the light of these messages by means of a questionnaire. Then, in Chapter 9, we will describe the ways in which these different types of decisions are likely to be experienced by your personality in your daily life.

However, just before we come to the questionnaire that will reveal *your* personality type, some readers may like to rise to the challenge of discovering their own unique decisions. This is how to go about it: Think back to the experiences of your childhood that in some way seem to have marked important turning points for you. Some common turning points are: starting school, moving house, the birth of a younger brother or sister, the death of a grandparent or other loved person, the separation or divorce of parents, gaining a step-parent. For each of these experiences ask yourself, How did I feel? What did I think? What *sense* did I make of it? A summary one-sentence answer to these questions will probably represent *one of your unique decisions about life.*

One very important decision that all of us make concerns *how we relate to people in general.* Although it may seem far-fetched, this decision is revealed in what we remember being told about our births. However, it requires a bit of an imaginative leap to translate the literal statement about your birth into the psychological statement about the way you tend to relate to other people. A few examples may help.

'My mother had an easy labour and everyone was very happy' probably means: 'I relate easily and happily to other people.'
'I nearly died' probably means: 'I tend to feel very badly hurt in my relationships.'
'My mother nearly died' probably means: 'Other people get very badly hurt by their relationships to me.'

When I was first told by a colleague how profoundly revealing of the general nature of a person's relationship the story of his or her birth could be, I was somewhat skeptical. Yet, almost without exception, in the many 'translations' I have made of people's birth stories, they and I have been amazed at the exactitude with which such a translation reflects the essential pattern of that person's relationships with other people. It is not a matter of the objective reality of his birth forming his decisions; rather it is his decision which influences him to remember the facts which best fit the decision. (On occasions, I have actually heard parents refute the 'facts' – and the telling of them – that their children are 'certain' they were told.)

The best way to validate (or invalidate) the relevance of birth stories to relationships is to test it for yourself. However, to do so requires that you give yourself permission to make free and imaginative use of metaphors. Let me share with you my own birth story and how I understand it to reflect some core features of my relationships. I remember being told that I was born on a Friday evening. My mother had worked hard all day cleaning the house and cooking for the weekend. She had just finished her work and set the table for dinner for herself and my father, when she went into labour and I was born quickly and easily.

The core elements in the general tenor of all my relationships that are reflected in this story are that I am only able to enjoy myself and get what I want for myself when I have done my duty by others. Then I am able to get what I want 'quickly and easily.' Even at a literal level, the story of my birth is pertinent to my life. I have always – essentially unconsciously – crammed most of my domestic responsibilities into Fridays, and my now nearly grown-up children have difficulty persuading me that it is all right sometimes for me to go out and enjoy myself without feeling obliged first to cook their dinner.

At this point you may be prompted to respond, 'Very interesting, but so what?' The point is that, now the decision is conscious, I am able to take responsibility for those aspects of my relationships which reflect it. The humour of the recognition of my decision also enables me – occasionally! – to forgo some of my previous rigid adherence to it, since I now appreciate it as having 'absolute' value only because I have made it so.

The same advantages apply to all our decisions that we are able to bring into conscious awareness. Being conscious of and having a sense of humour about our decisions may also profoundly facilitate us in achieving the important virtue of tolerance.

In rcsponse to the question, 'What do you know about the day you were born?' some people reply, 'Nothing.' From my experience, this reply implies, with a high degree of reliability, that the person making this claim is in some important way ignorant of the general nature of his relationships. However, a little prompting will usually enable these people to reveal some knowledge they do have. Even if they know nothing about the day of their birth, they probably do know something about their mother's pregnancy with them, or the reactions of various people to their birth, and this knowledge may be very pertinent to the quality of their relationships to others.

A woman I once met told me, 'When my mother was pregnant with me she could eat hardly any foods. But there were a few foods like oranges and liver pâté that she really loved.' I offered her the hypothesis that she didn't get on well with most people, but she had a few close friends whom she loved very much. She immediately confirmed the validity of my interpretation.

And a paranoic young man told me, 'When I was born they held me upside down and I cried and they all laughed.'

Now it's your turn.

DISCOVER YOUR PERSONALITY TYPE

Remember back to Chapter 5, where we discovered that all the possible painful Adapted Child messages we may receive from our parents tend to fall into five broad categories:

> Don't feel you are good enough.
> Don't ask for things for yourself.

Don't succeed.
Don't be yourself.
Don't feel you belong.

Just as all *painful messages* fall into five broad categories, so all our *painful decisions* around these messages fall into five broad categories. Each of the general types of painful message has its corresponding general type of painful decision.

Remember, too, that in Chapter 7 it was argued that the receipt of painful messages is an inevitable part of being human and that particular painful messages tend to be endemic in particular families and to get passed on from one generation to the next to the next. . . . It was also argued that, at a deep level, parents are actually ashamed of passing on their Adapted Child hang-ups to their children, and so tend to reserve these transactions for the privacy of intimate family life.

However, since all of us are bound to receive and to pass on to our own children some painful messages, society as a whole has developed some socially approved devices that enable parents to transmit painful messages to their children *in public and without shame.* In this way, each of the five broad categories of painful message and its associated painful decision has a corresponding device that enables an individual to confirm his painful decisions under cover, as it were. Although every individual is bound to set his life up to confirm his painful (and pleasurable) decisions over and over again, even without benefit of these socially sanctioned devices, these devices provide efficient and camouflaging ways for him to do so.

The next chapter is devoted to the exposure of these socially approved behaviours and the decisions they serve that cause us pain. You will almost certainly immediately recognize each of the syndromes as 'typical' either of yourself or of someone you know, since these ways of behaving and their associated decisions are so universal and pervasive in everyday life.

Although each person's 'personality' is defined in this book as the sum total of all the permissions, inhibitions and decisions in his Child ego state, since behaviours leading to the confirmation of painful decisions are so commonplace in everyday life, I have chosen to call the five syndromes that serve painful decisions five 'personality types'. Strictly speaking, they are five Adapted Child types.

In everyday life, we all exhibit some of the behaviours and attitudes of each of the 'personality types' described in Chapter 9 some of the time. However, each of us tends to exhibit a couple of these types of behaviour much more often than the others, since they most efficiently serve our own particular painful decisions. Although you are unlikely to have any difficulty in recognizing your own typical behaviours and attitudes from the descriptions, the following questionnaire may provide useful confirmation if you are in doubt. Each of the five syndromes has four questions relevant to it and, at the end of the questionnaire, the five personality types are named alongside the numbers of the questions that refer to them. Answer YES or NO to each question. If you find it impossible to decide one way or the other for any reason, put a question mark.

1. Are you an only child or the youngest child in your family?
2. When things go wrong do you tend to feel guilty?
3. Do you quite often feel a failure?
4. Do you quite often feel life is futile?
5. Were either of your parents Roman Catholic or Jewish or regular churchgoers of any other denomination?

6. Were you separated from your parents before you were six? E. g. by being hospitalized or fostered or by being looked after by a relative or nanny while your parents were away.
7. Did either of your parents have ambitions they were prevented from fulfilling through lack of opportunity?
8. Do you quite often feel you would like to get closer to other people than you do?
9. Were either of your parents quite often concerned about what other people – e. g. the neighbours – thought of them?
10. Did you go to boarding school?
11. When things go wrong do you tend to feel unappreciated?
12. When things go wrong do you tend to feel embarrassed?
13. Did you have a lot of responsibility – e. g. looking after younger brothers or sisters – when you were growing up?
14. Do you quite often feel nobody lets you be yourself?
15. When things go wrong do you tend to feel you can't be bothered trying any more?
16. When things go wrong do you tend to panic and feel you can't think straight?
17. Did either of your parents need a lot of looking after or special consideration when you were a child? E. g. through chronic illness or depression.
18. Are you a perfectionist?
19. Do you quite often feel worthless?
20. Do you compare yourself to other people a lot?

Scoring: Score one point for each YES answer. Score half a

point for each QUESTION MARK. A NO answer scores nil. If you score two or more points in any category this means that that *personality type* is a prominent part of your Adapted Child. Some people belong to only one type and some people have all five types prominent in their Adapted Child ego states. But people usually find that they belong mostly to two types.

The Perfectionist: 2, 5, 18, 19
The Stiff Upper Lipper: 8, 11, 13, 17
The Try Harder: 3, 7, 15, 20
The Doormat: 1, 9, 12, 14
The Hurrier: 4, 6, 10, 16

The Perfectionist is associated with the Adapted Child message, 'Don't feel you are good enough,' and serves the general decision, 'I am worthless;' the Stiff Upper Lipper is associated with the Adapted Child message, 'Don't ask for things for yourself,' and serves the general decision, 'I am unloveworthy;' the Try Harder is associated with the Adapted Child message, 'Don't succeed' and serves the general decision 'I am not as good as I think I am; the Doormat is associated with the Adapted Child message, 'Don't be yourself,' and serves the general decision, 'I am misunderstood;' and the Hurrier is associated with the Adapted Child message, 'Don't belong,' and serves the general decision, 'I am an outsider.'

CHAPTER NINE

Five Personality Types – Know Your Adapted Child

Society, recognizing the reality that all human beings seek pain as well as pleasure, gives its approval to certain behaviours and attitudes which enable and lead people to reaffirm their painful decisions. There are five such recognizable syndromes of behaviours and attitudes, corresponding to the five general categories of painful payoffs, and they are so pervasive in people's everyday lives that they are recognizable as five 'personality types'.

The five personality types – the Perfectionist, the Stiff Upper Lipper, the Try Harder, the Doormat and the Hurrier – are described in terms of the typical decisions they serve and the kinds of Adapted Child messages that support them, general traits that are typical of each of them, and permissions needed for each of them to overcome the pains associated with the decisions they serve. A summary table is given of the most common words and body language associated with each of the five personality types (p.122).

HOW SOCIETY SANCTIONS THE ADAPTED CHILD

Society, by virtue of its institutions and its laws, is grandparent to us all. Explicitly, it is most readily recognizable as exerting Parent control and constraint on the anarchic impulses of our unbridled, self-centred Free Child. It does not allow us – without punishment – to take or damage other people's property or hurt other people; and, to some extent, with Government Warnings and censorship of various kinds, it also does its best to prevent us from hurting ourselves. And it nurtures us with child, old age and other monetary benefits as well as municipal housing and subsidized medicine.

From its Adult, society provides us with such facilities as schools and universities and banks and town halls to help us gain and maintain the necessary skills we need to look after ourselves effectively as independent and autonomous grown-ups.

From its Free Child, it gives us the major *permissions* of free speech, the rights to protest and strike, to bring our children up according to our own lights, with minimal interference, to worship as we wish, to vote for our (Parent) government . . . and a host of other implicit, lesser freedoms of which we are generally unaware until we compare our lives to the lives of people living in more Parent-dominated societies.

And, most subtly of all, society also transmits Adapted Child messages in accordance with its own profound (but largely unconscious) knowledge that, having been cast out of paradise, we are all inevitably committed to experiencing life as painful as well as joyous. Recognizing this reality and understanding our unwillingness to accept responsibility for our pains, society has devised for us some approved ways of reaffirming our painful decisions under the guise of *pseudo-Parent 'virtues'*. These 'virtues' *beguile us into believing we are behaving in ways conducive to our happiness, but, in fact, they all lead us inexorably down fast and slippery slopes to our most painful decisions.*

Although we are each committed to reaffirming our painful (and pleasurable) decisions over and over again, irrespective of how many and difficult psychological contortions we may need to use to do so, *the five socially sanctioned 'personality types' provide us with very efficient short-cuts to reaffirming the five broad categories of painful decisions.* From start to finish, the process of 'virtue-to-pain' may take as little as a few seconds and usually takes no more than a few minutes.

The five general 'virtues' are 'being a perfectionist', 'being stoical' (the Stiff Upper Lipper), 'trying hard', 'being nice' (the Doormat), and 'hurrying up'.

Because they are so subtly camouflaged as Parent virtues, we all tend to defend these Adapted Child invitations to misery as if they really were virtues – especially the ones that are most prominent in our own Adapted Child! But there is all the difference in the world between aiming for perfection (and ending up with a worthless mess) and doing your very best (and ending up feeling pleased with the result); all the difference in the world between hiding your painful feelings (and ending up feeling lonely and rejected) and having courage in the face of acknowledged pain; all the difference in the world between 'trying hard' (and ending up copping-out or otherwise failing) and determinedly seeing a task through to its completion; all the difference in the world between 'doing the right thing' (and ending up displeasing yourself or others) and really considering other people's feelings and wishes and expecting them also to consider yours; and all the difference in the world between rushing (and ending up panicking and late and left out of things) and getting on with things without wasting time.

Sadly, for many people the stereotyped Adapted Child behaviours and attitudes leading to the confirmation of painful decisions are central to nearly all their social transactions. Precise estimates vary, but all Transactional Analysts agree that such essentially maladaptive, hurtful, get-nowhere behaviour dominates most people's lives.

However, awareness is three-quarters of the way to control, and it is hoped that readers of this book will gain much awareness that will enable them to choose, not only a mate, but increased authenticity and freedom from pain in their lives in general. As Eric Berne put it in his famous book, *Games People Play*, 'There may be no hope for the human race, but there is hope for individual members of it.'

THE PERFECTIONIST

The Perfectionist is seeking to reaffirm a decision like, 'I am not good enough,' or, 'I am a worthless sinner.'

The Perfectionist is often created in a religious family. Even when not religiously observant, a Roman Catholic or Jewish family almost always predisposes a child to have a Perfectionist-type Adapted Child. The Perfectionist is very moralistic and often goes with a 'whole self' that is dominated by the Parent ego state. Typical messages received are, 'Don't give in to temptation,' 'Don't be carefree,' 'Don't take chances,' 'Don't be tolerant.'

The personality characteristics that help the Perfectionist to prove her fundamental decision include feeling guilty, making a total mess of things, being punctilious in action and over-precise in speech; being nit-picking in argument and fault-finding of others' character or performance on the job. She is the one who always (or never) steps on the lines of the pavement, who never walks under a ladder, and always waits for her train on exactly the same spot on the platform, and double-checks that the door is locked and all the gas taps off before she goes to bed. Not surprisingly, she has a tendency to be depressed. Overall, she fears some terrible consequences if she falls short of perfection. When she projects her Adapted Child outwards onto other people to the extent of always finding something to criticize, she invokes irritation and anger in others. But those Perfectionists who seem mostly to direct their criticism onto themselves often invoke others to feel sorry for them for the obvious pain they cause themselves.

The Perfectionist will paint a room with meticulous care but, when he has finished, will scrutinize his work and discover a tiny unpainted spot in the North-West corner of the ceiling. He is likely to keep the spot squintingly in focus as he approaches the ladder, wielding the paint brush, only to trip over the tin of paint on the floor and spend the next two hours cleaning up the mess he has made.

The Perfectionist needs most of all to acquire permission to accept that there are a very large number of worthwhile attributes and values – apart from his own – that people may have.

THE STIFF UPPER LIPPER

The Stiff Upper Lipper is seeking to reaffirm a decision like, 'I am unappreciated,' or, 'I am not worthy of love.'

The Stiff Upper Lipper is a very British type of Adapted Child. His family background is usually one where children are expected to be seen but not heard, and the sooner they grow up the better. Expressing emotion – particularly painful emotion – and kissing and cuddling are positively discouraged. This Adapted Child often goes with a 'whole self' dominated by the Adult. Typical messages received are, 'Don't be a child,' 'Don't ask things for yourself,' 'Don't be warm,' 'Don't be close,' 'Don't show your feelings,' 'Don't lose your dignity.'

The characteristics that help the Stiff Upper Lipper to prove her fundamental decision include 'pulling her socks up', asking for things in such a way that she won't be given them, being stand-offish, being bored, feeling unappreciated, not revealing her feelings, being brave and stoical, always looking after others' needs but neglecting her own. It is the Stiff Upper Lipper who commands a regiment and leads his men into battle, who is marvellous in a crisis, gets on with things, goes for brisk walks and gets up a 6 a. m. to go for an early morning swim every day of the year. He never cries or whines or complains, and often wears a moustache to keep his upper lip hidden, just in case, despite his best efforts, it should slacken. Overall, the Stiff Upper Lipper is deeply lonely and stroke-deprived, but to others he usually appears aloof and stand-offish.

If the Stiff Upper Lipper just misses a bus, but manages to catch up with it when it is stopped at the traffic lights just ahead of the bus stop, she is unlikely to indicate to the driver her wish to get on. Desperately in a hurry as she may be, she would rather be late than risk the humiliation of knocking on the door to get the driver to let her on, only to be ignored.

The Stiff Upper Lipper needs most of all to gain permission to ask for things for his own Child, and to realize that everybody's requests are rejected some of the time. Only by asking for what he wants and giving himself permission to be rejected sometimes, will he ever give people the opportunity also to accept him and give him what he wants the rest of the time.

THE TRY HARDER

The Try Harder is seeking to reaffirm a decision like, 'I'm a failure', or, 'I'm not as good as I think I am.'

Try Harders usually come from families where parents are resentful or bitter about their lot and blame other people or society for the fact that they have not got what they wanted in life. Children who grow up to be Try Harders are not allowed to be pleased with themselves; if they dare to achieve things and be proud of the fact, they are quickly put down with, 'Who do you think you are?' Typical messages received are, 'Don't succeed,' 'Don't be pleased with yourself,' 'Don't do better than I did,' 'Don't get what you want,' 'Don't be confident,' 'Don't be ambitious.'

The personality characteristics that help the Try Harder to prove his fundamental decision include giving up very quickly, feeling frightened of failure, having grandiose ideas of his own worth, putting other people down, calling other people lucky and himself unlucky, putting all his eggs in one basket, being competitive, constantly comparing himself to others as being inferior or superior to them, copping out by saying, 'I can't be bothered.' Overall, he can't bear to face his parents' jealousy of him if he should succeed in a way they wanted to but didn't. Other people see the Try Harder as conceited.

The Try Harder buys a ticket in a lottery and excitedly thinks of nothing else but winning until the lottery is drawn. She may decide to enter her baby in a Beautiful Baby Competition and expect her baby to win, but when she gets there and sees all the other babies, she fears her baby might not win, and so changes her mind and doesn't enter her. Later, she compares her baby to the winner and thinks her baby much more beautiful.

The Try Harder needs most of all to gain permission to realize that everybody fails some of the time. Only by giving herself permission to see set-backs as inevitable along the way, will she be able, in due course, to achieve overall success. She needs to appreciate that, fundamentally, all human beings are equal.

THE DOORMAT

The Doormat is seeking to reaffirm a decision like, 'Nobody lets me be myself,' or, 'I'm misunderstood.'

Doormats usually come from families where respectability is emphasized and expression of Free Child wishes or feelings – especially bad feelings like jealousy, anger, vengeance or hatred – are considered an embarrassment. 'What will the neighbours think?' rules such families' lives. Any authentic expression of feeling on the part of the child is likely to be responded to with, 'That's not nice.' Overall, these parents treat their children like accessories that improve their own appearance. But so long as a child responds obediently to such parents by only feeling and doing what they tell him to feel and do, he is rewarded by having all his Adapted Child wishes granted before he is even aware of having them. This is the spoilt child – spoilt in a deeper sense than the obvious one of being over-indulged. Only children almost inevitably have this Adapted Child prominent in their personalities, and a youngest child or any child that, for some reason, is the 'apple of a parent's eye' is also prone to be a Doormat. Typical messages received are, 'Don't feel what you feel, but what I tell you to feel,' 'Don't leave me,' 'Don't grow up,' 'Don't express bad feelings,' 'Don't know what you want.'

The personality characteristics that help the Doormat to prove his fundamental decision include being overly nice and polite, bursting out with resentful hostility and rudeness quite inappropriately, telling other people what they (other people) feel, bossing other people around, getting other people to tell them what to do, never expressing dislike of anybody. Overall, they see relationships in terms of control. Sometimes they seek and submit to other people's control of them, and at other times they see it as their turn to control other people. Other people feel they don't know where they stand with Doormats.

A typical conversation with a doormat may go like this:
YOU: Would you like a cup of tea or coffee?
DOORMAT: That would be very nice.
YOU: Which would you prefer, tea or coffee?
DOORMAT: Whatever's easier.
YOU: It's all the same – a teabag or instant coffee.
DOORMAT: I'll have whatever you're having.
Whichever you make, chances are he would have preferred the other and resents you for not having read his mind.

The Doormat needs most of all to gain permission to know what she feels and to express her feelings openly, including what she wants and how she genuinely feels about people, without being either 'polite' or 'rude'.

THE HURRIER

The Hurrier is seeking to reaffirm a decision like, 'I don't belong,' or, 'I can't think.'

Hurriers come from families where there is a lot of tension in the air. Such families bicker and screech and shout at each other and rush around frenetically. Things are generally disorganized and chaotic and, from the child's point of view, frighteningly unpredictable. Nobody has time to give the child many strokes at all, and those he does get are mostly angry negative ones. The child is treated by the parents as an object that gets tripped over. As often as possible they get him out of the way, so they don't have to notice him at all. If they are rich, they employ a nanny and send him to boarding school. Overall, the child learns that his choice is between complying instantly with the orders shouted at him or being left out of things completely. If he complies, he gives up all chance of thinking for himself; if he takes his time and thinks before acting, by the time he does act, everybody else has moved on to something else and he is left alone and ignored. Typical messages received are, 'Don't belong,' (Note the similarity to, 'Don't be long'), 'Don't think,' 'Don't exist,' 'Don't take your time,' 'Don't be sane,' 'Don't be a nuisance.'

The personality characteristics that help the Hurrier to prove his fundamental decision include always being in a hurry, being frightened or anxious, being late and generally unreliable, panicking, being tired, (often to the point of falling asleep in company), being immobilized by apathy, tapping his feet with impatience, frowning in non-comprehension of what others are saying, not allowing others to finish what they are saying. He is fidgety in company and gives the impression that he would rather be somewhere else than with you. He sees life as futile and is basically self-destructive, which he may express through being accident-prone, driving dangerously, drinking too much or taking drugs. Other people generally react to the Hurrier by feeling tired or getting a headache.

The Hurrier may accept invitations to three different New Year's Eve parties. He will arrive at the first one very early and leave it, just as things are warming up, to go on to the second. While he is at the second party, supper is served, but he doesn't have any, thinking he'll save his appetite for when he gets to the third party. Meanwhile, he feels left out of things while everybody else is eating. He goes on to the third party, where all the food and most of the drink has gone, and everybody is already paired off in intimate huddles.

The Hurrier needs most of all to gain permission to realize that love is not a matter of 'all or nothing' and that something in between is worth having. She needs to gain permission to use her Adult and to belong amongst people by not rejecting them, and learning to say 'We' as well as 'I'.

HOW TO RECOGNIZE THE PERSONALITY TYPES IN FIVE MINUTES

The five personality types are everywhere around us and constantly influence our dealings with other people in our everyday lives. Knowing the types of Adapted Child in other people as well as ourselves may enable us, through heightened awareness, to avoid some of our own most painful decisions and, incidentally, help others avoid their most painful decisions. The Adapted Child ego state is very contagious; one person beginning a conversation from his or her Adapted Child almost inevitably prompts the other person into her or his Adapted Child. Refusing to respond to people's invitations to give them their target negative strokes is a very good way of helping increase the overall happiness of the world.

In Chapters 10 and 11 we will see that there are ways of positively bringing out the best in each of the types. Meanwhile, to help avoid bringing out the worst in yourself and others, the table below summarizes the most common words and body language of each of the personality types. See if you can, through your own observations of yourself and others, expand this table for your own use.

PERSONALITY TYPE	WORDS	BODY LANGUAGE
THE PERFECTIONIST	perfect/worthless; clean/dirty; guilty; tidy/untidy; should/shouldn't; obviously; as it were; of course; actually; precisely; Nobody's perfect; It's not my fault; . . . for my sins . . . Good Heavens!	precision; over-qualification; won't be interrupted; itemizes and numbers points while he is talking; purses bottom lip between forefinger and thumb before speaking.
THE STIFF UPPER LIPPER	weakness/strength; boring; Pull yourself together! I don't care; No comment; It's no good crying over spilt milk; You don't appreciate what I'm saying/doing; says 'one' instead of 'I'.	over-straight back; legs crossed; has moustache; pulls socks up; straightens tie; appears to be Adult all the time (but often actually in Adapted Child); cracks joints of fingers.
THE DOORMAT	Dear; Really? nice; super; Y'know; I mean; embarrassed; Please yourself! You misunderstand me.	nods head; raises eyebrows; runs fingers through hair (men); horizontal lines on forehead; questioning inflexion.
THE TRY HARDER	I'll try; could/couldn't; impossible; superior/inferior; fail/succeed; I don't know; it's hard; I'm better than/not as good as you/him/her.	sits forward, elbows on legs, chin in hand; puzzled look; asks more than one question at a time; does not answer question asked; stutters.
THE HURRIER	Hurry up; panic; anxiety; quickly; energy, time, tired, crazy; It's pointless; It's futile; I haven't got time.	brows knitted into vertical lines between the eyes; speaks rapidly and interrupts himself and others; fidgety; breathless; eyes shifty; taps fingers or feet.

CHAPTER TEN

Types of Couples – Truth or Consequences

Although the 'five personality types' of the Adapted Child are primarily devices which provide us with short-cuts to re-affirming our most painful decisions, the Adapted Child traits can also be transformed into genuine and valuable virtues and skills.

There are fifteen possible pairings of the five Adapted Child types. How each type tends to be expressed in personal relationships varies according to the type of Adapted Child expressed by the other person.

THE BETTER HALF OF YOUR ADAPTED CHILD

Now that we have established the five syndromes of attitudes and behaviours through which we all subversively reinforce our painful decisions, we need to know how we can use this knowledge of people in general and ourselves in particular better to choose a mate. We have three options in deciding what use to make of our knowledge of the Adapted Child.

The ideal use of our knowledge of the five Adapted Child syndromes would be to eliminate them completely from the repertoire of our responses to the world and to other people and replace them with authentic and spontaneous responses from our Parent, Adult or Free Child, in accordance only with the unique reality of each moment as it offers itself for our experience. This option is unrealistic since, as we have seen, at least some painful decisions are inescapably part of being human and we will inevitably, one way or another, find devices to reinforce these decisions.

Our second option is to deny the pervasive compulsiveness and nastiness of the Adapted Child in our lives and thus hope to avoid it. In this we would be behaving like the person who refuses to go to the doctor because she fears the diagnosis, and acts as if by ignoring her symptoms she will remain well, whereas by attending to them she will become ill. Transparently foolish as this attitude is, it is the creed by which most people live out their relationships and their lives. Essentially, this response is an expression of a confused attitude towards 'free will' and 'fate'; in the name of 'free will' painful reality is denied, and in the name of 'fate' responsibility for the consequences of this denial is evaded.

Our third option is to see ourselves as to a large extent bound by the determinism of the messages we received and the decisions we made around these messages in childhood, but as also having some freedom (gained through *Adult awareness*) to modify the effects these messages and decisions have on our lives. This option expresses the central philosophy and theme of this book.

Empowered by our Adult knowledge of human nature in general and our own unique individuality in particular, there are two separate ways in which we may use our free will to enhance our lives.

We can *choose*, hour by hour, minute by minute, which ego state we are going to be in, instead of reacting automatically and compulsively. Although there will always be certain situations and certain people in our lives powerful enough to invoke our Adapted Child even against our will, by conscious awareness and control of their ego states most people can succeed in significantly reducing the frequency and intensity of their Adapted Child responses.

Secondly, we can actually make our Adapted Child ego states work for rather than against our happiness. This possibility derives from the fact that each of the Adapted Child personality types deploys its own pseudo-Adult or pseudo-Parent behaviours to achieve its unhappy payoffs. While they are serving to reinforce unhappy decisions, these behaviours are, by definition, hypocritical and false, but with a slight *change of mind* the same behaviour can be transformed into true Parent and Adult virtues and skills.

If careful attention is paid to *the words people use* it is possible to discern, with a high degree of reliability, the difference between words which are leading a person to reaffirm a painful decision and similar words which are authentic and oriented to true satisfaction. With a little practice, it becomes possible to discriminate quite easily the subtle differences in the quality of the words a person chooses to use when he is in his Adapted Child as compared with the words he chooses to use when he is in any of his other ego states. The table on page 122 is designed to help the reader tune into the words associated with each of the five types of Adapted Child behaviour leading to unhappy endings, but we have not yet mentioned the words that describe the authentic skills and virtues into which these behaviours may be transformed. Can you guess which personality type is best equipped to practise each of the following skills and virtues? (You will find the answers later in this chapter.)

1. Flexibility
2. Efficiency
3. Reliability
4. Organization
5. Persistence

Say these words aloud to yourself and feel how positive they are compared with the Adapted Child words listed in the table on page 122. Think of how much human achievement is dependent on these traits, yet their existence in human nature is a direct consequence of the re-deployment of Adapted Child energy! Shakespeare knew it when he said:

> They say best men are moulded out of faults,
> And, for the most, become much more the better
> For being a little bad.

(Answers to quiz above: 1. The Doormat. 2. The Hurrier 3. The Stiff Upper Lipper 4. The Perfectionist 5. The Try Harder)

TYPES OF COUPLES

Choosing a mate for maximum overall happiness is clearly a complex matter. In Chapters 11 and 12 we will be simplifying this complexity by delineating the kinds of sub-choices involved in the overall decision. But from all that has so far been said it should by now be clear that your Adapted Child in relation to your mate's Adapted Child is of overwhelming importance in predicting the long-term happiness or unhappiness that you will find with each other. The natural bias of a courtship relationship is towards a predominance of Free Child to Free Child transactions between you, but sooner or later – and usually sooner! – the realities of yours and his or her Adapted Child will make themselves felt and will need to be faced if you are to continue to be happy with each other.

For this reason it seems a good idea, before concluding this book, to give the reader a brief idea of what to expect of the various possibilities of Adapted Child to Adapted Child couplings. Each of the five Adapted Child types can relate to any other Adapted Child type as well as to its own type. So, theoretically, there are fifteen possible relationships between the Adapted Child of one person and the Adapted Child of another – five relationships between similar types and ten relationships between different types.

In reality, though, it is rarely sufficient to know your Adapted Child to Adapted Child relationship in terms of only one type in you and one type in your mate. In most people's Adapted Child *two* types predominate in approximately equal measure. So you are likely to find your and your mate's Adapted Child relationship described in four of the fifteen possible categories rather than one. For example, let's say your Adapted Child is predominantly a Perfectionist and a Hurrier, whereas your mate's Adapted Child is predominantly a Stiff Upper Lipper and a Hurrier. Sometimes you will relate Perfectionist to Stiff Upper Lipper, sometimes Perfectionist to Hurrier, sometimes Hurrier to Stiff Upper Lipper, and sometimes Hurrier to Hurrier – and these experiences will be very different from each other!

There will also be times when you will observe in yourself or your mate behaviour which seems to blend traits from more than one of the types of Adapted Child. In fact, this is very often the reason why people tend to have two types rather than one prominent in their personalities. It quite often seems to be the case that one of the types is not sufficient on its own to serve the particular decision the individual is seeking to reinforce, so he combines two types to provide himself with a more powerful device for achieving the payoff he is seeking. For example, it is often the case that people who have decisions like, 'People hurt you if you give them the chance,' will express the Try Harder and the Hurrier together because the typical behaviour and attitudes of each of these types combines particularly well with the other to 'prove' such a decision. Or somebody with an, 'I must be good for people to like me,' kind of decision may well combine Perfectionist and Doormat characteristics to 'prove' this position.

It is important for the reader to remember that *the 'five personality types' are not ends but means* to the end of reaffirming painful decisions. It is easy to slip into thinking of the five types as being descriptions of what people 'are', in an intrinsic way, like being short and green-eyed and intelligent. Indeed, Adapted Child behaviours are so pervasive and apparently intransigent in all our lives that it is often a convenient mental shorthand to think of them as core truths about people. But they are not congenital, they are *learned ways of behaving* (when in our Adapted Child). The real core truths about us all are the *messages and decisions* we are obeying, to which the behaviours and attitudes of the five personality types are merely servants. With or without benefit of the Adapted Child syndromes we have called 'personality types' we will abide by and constantly seek to reaffirm our *decisions*, which are the true core of our being. It is best always to keep in mind that the 'five personality types' are merely *five socially-approved short-cuts to reinforcing our painful decisions under the guise of pseudo-virtuous behaviour*.

In the descriptions which follow of the nature of the fifteen possible Adapted Child to Adapted Child relationships it is my intention to give the reader the general flavour of what to expect from each of the pairings. There are very many ways in which each of the five Adapted Child syndromes may be expressed in everyday life, so the usefulness of my descriptions will depend on the reader's willingness to translate my comments imaginatively into the realm of his or her own experience. The Perfectionist, for example, may equally express himself through being an accountant or a preacher or a meticulous housewife. The Stiff Upper Lipper may find expression for her Adapted Child needs in occupations as diverse as being a solo yachtsman or a psychotherapist. The Try Harder may form a new political party with a view to creating a revolution, or buy a metal detector with the aim of finding gold. The Doormat may find an outlet for her Adapted Child in being an actress or in working for a large organization where she can be assured always of being both boss and subordinate. And the Hurrier may find satisfaction in being an ambulance driver or a travelling salesman or an air traffic controller.

Parallel to all these many possible ways in which people may express their Adapted Child healthily through their occupations, there are as many and diverse ways in which people may express their Adapted Child both constructively and destructively in personal relationships. The descriptions that follow are generalizations from what I have learned in analyzing the meanings of the Adapted Child relationships of many people, but they are in no way intended to be read as dogmatic statements of fact. Nonetheless, I hope that many of my comments reflect sufficiently commonplace experience that the reader will, in many cases, readily match his or her own observations to mine.

The Perfectionist and the Perfectionist. Like most couplings of like-to-like, this pair probably get on well with each other. They are apt to be united by their *common beliefs* and, so long as they do not disagree fundamentally about what is and what is not important in life, they give each other the security of feeling 'right' about things. Their life together tends to be ritualistic and extremely well organized and ordered. If they do disagree fundamentally about their values in life, they will frequently get on each other's nerves and will bicker and criticize each other interminably.

The Stiff Upper Lipper and the Stiff Upper Lipper. This relationship is characterized by a great deal of *mutual independence* between the partners. Each is especially averse to what they would call 'emotional suffocation', so they support each other in mutual understanding of the other's need for privacy. So long as they both have important interests outside as well as within their relationship they get on very well together. If one of them does not have an important interest outside the relationship he or she will be resentful of the lack of time given to the relationship by the other. One will feel neglected and the other 'suffocated'.

The Try Harder and the Try Harder. Of all the like-to-like relationships between Adapted Child ego states this is the one least likely to work for the general benefit of both partners. At best, this couple may be united in *hostility and envy* towards most other people, which may, for example, find expression in their working together for a lost cause. However, it is more often the case that their relationship is based on one partner chronically criticizing the other in order to boost his or her own very precarious self-esteem. In such a relationship each partner will secretly sabotage the other's achievement of his or her ambitions; they are both constantly on tenterhooks lest the other 'win' over them in some way or other. Life for them is one long competition.

The Doormat and the Doormat. This couple is usually united in a very stable relationship of *mutual dependence.* Each of the partners is secretly terrified of being left alone and so they are both rigidly obedient to their unspoken agreement that they will each be and behave towards the other in the ways the other demands. In this way they both achieve the *emotional security* they crave above all else. The price they pay for this is the stifling of spontaneity and authentic expression of emotion. Neither risks offending the other and so disturbing the safe equilibrium of the relationship. Sometimes this relationship continues on a conventional and even keel for a lifetime; sometimes such a couple punctuates the essential politeness of the relationship with periodic angry quarrels which release (though often unconsciously) the built-up resentment each feels for his or her dependence on the other.

The Hurrier and the Hurrier. Since the core attitude of the Hurrier in relationship to others is, 'I'll reject you before you can reject me,' this relationship is so unstable that it is unlikely to be formed at all between two people who are both principally Hurriers. When Hurrier to Hurrier is a minor component of a couple's relationship, it will probably find expression in either or both of them slamming out of the house without saying where they are going or for how long. Sometimes they may get drunk or 'stoned out of their minds' in each other's company, but the isolation each of them then feels is as great as it would be if they were each alone.

The Perfectionist and the Stiff Upper Lipper. This couple is usually united by a *puritanical attitude to life.* They are often both ambitious and work very hard to achieve their goals. The Perfectionist easily accommodates to the Stiff Upper Lipper's view that 'reliability is the better part of love,' and the Stiff Upper Lipper pleases the Perfectionist by being willing to 'get on with things' without complaining. They are likely to enjoy conversations with each other which are both serious and playfully critical and ironical. They are unlikely to cause each other pain, but they do tend to reinforce rather than positively modify each other's essential rigidity.

The Perfectionist and the Try Harder. This is often an obviously unhappy relationship based on *open warfare.* Both are very critical of each other, but the Perfectionist, who tends to be the more intelligent in this partnership, is usually the one who, in arguments, consistently ends up being the Persecuting victor while the Try Harder ends up being the humiliated victim. The Perfectionist is using the Try Harder to project his own feeling of worthlessness out of himself, while the Try Harder is continually reinforced in her fundamental position of, 'No matter how hard I try I'll never be good enough.' The Perfectionist often threatens to leave the Try Harder, but he secretly knows he is dependent on the Try Harder for his needed feeling of 'superiority', and both know their relationship is likely to continue in its unhappiness for a very long time.

The Perfectionist and the Doormat. This is often a very stable and contented relationship based on agreed *dominance and submission roles.* The Perfectionist is the boss and the Doormat is happily obedient. The Perfectionist's quest for having things be and be done exactly the way she wants is fulfilled and, complementarily, the Doormat is profoundly reassured in knowing he is doing the 'right' and 'good' things (as dictated by the Perfectionist). However, because of their contented equilibrium, the Perfectionist tends to lack any stimulating challenge to her rigidity of outlook and the Doormat gains no permission to live outside the bounds of being 'too good to be true'. Sometimes such couples find periodic expression of the suppressed side of the Adapted Child in each of them through episodes in which the Doormat expresses some fleeting defiant rebelliousness and the Perfectionist responds with angry criticism. However, the Perfectionist quickly controls the outburst of the Doormat and things usually return rapidly to their normal peace and calm.

The Perfectionist and the Hurrier. At the profoundest levels of their personalities the individuals who form this couple are supremely well-matched. When referred to the deepest psychological level, the Perfectionist and the Hurrier are expressions of *the fear of death and the wish for death* respectively. To this extent the Perfectionist is a cowardly stick-in-the-mud and the Hurrier a brazen dare-devil. They are capable of cancelling out the unhealthy extreme that each on its own stands for and creating, instead, in their relationship an optimally healthy balance between organization and efficiency, thrift and extravagance, caution and daring, structure and spontaneity . . . and many other adaptive compromises between a wide range of polarities in life. Transactionally, the Perfectionist tends to play the role of sometimes indulgent and sometimes controlling Parent to the sometimes charming and sometimes exasperating Child of the Hurrier. The only possibility of serious harm in this relationship arises when one or both express their Adapted Child at a very high pitch. When this occurs, the two Adapted Child ego states may escalate each other in a vicious spiral until they lose their separate indentities and collide in insanity. (But in most of these couples such occurrences are very rare indeed.)

The Stiff Upper Lipper and the Try Harder. This is a relationship between essentially incompatible types. They are so fundamentally incapable of gratifying each other that a long-term relationship is unlikely between two people who are predominantly the Stiff Upper Lipper and the Try Harder. When this Adapted Child interaction is a minor aspect of the total relationship between a couple, the Stiff Upper Lipper will adapt a stance of cold and bored aloofness towards the Try Harder and the Try Harder will feel envious and aggressive towards the Stiff Upper Lipper. The Stiff Upper Lipper finds the Try Harder 'a bore' for 'whining' and for generally wearing his heart on his sleeve, and the Try Harder envies the Stiff Upper Lipper his 'cool', which the Try Harder perceives himself as lacking because of insufficient 'luck' or 'opportunity'. In transacting with each other, the Stiff Upper Lipper generally limits himself to peremptory brush-offs to the Try Harder, and the Try Harder is consumed with frustration and rage.

The Stiff Upper Lipper and the Doormat. This is basically a deeply unhappy relationship, but one which often endures for a lifetime. It is very commonly the chief component of many English marriages, the husband usually being the Stiff Upper Lipper and the wife the Doormat. The trouble with this relationship is that it readily provides each of the partners with easy affirmation if his or her most painful decisions without providing any positive compensations. The Stiff Upper Lipper longs most of all to have his needs understood and met without his needing to give voice to them; the Doormat is dependent on another's instructions as to how to behave to please the other person. The Doormat asks the Stiff Upper Lipper to tell her what he wants her to be and to do; the Stiff Upper Lipper replies, 'I want you to be intimate with me in a spontaneous and authentic way, not according to instructions.' The Doormat accuses the Stiff Upper Lipper of being 'cold' and the Stiff Upper Lipper crawls further and further into his shell. The Stiff Upper Lipper 'proves' the impossibility of being loved for himself, the Doormat 'proves' she is a 'good' person who is misunderstood and so vilified as 'bad'.

The Stiff Upper Lipper and the Hurrier. This is probably the most painful relationship of all. Each of the partners is fundamentally seeking to prove the inevitability of *profound loneliness* and they powerfully support each other in fulfilling this quest. The relationship often begins with the Stiff Upper Lipper Rescuing the Victim Hurrier, but these roles are quickly succeeded by the Hurrier Persecuting and rejecting the Stiff Upper Lipper who then becomes Victim. The Stiff Upper Lipper confirms, 'No matter how much love and caring I offer another person I am unappreciated. The only reason that makes sense is that I am intrinsically unloveworthy.' The Hurrier 'proves', 'It's futile forming a relationship. Other people never give me what I need, so it's best not to ask for love and to refuse any that is offered because it won't be enough and it won't last long anyway.' At the deepest levels of their personalities, the Stiff Upper Lipper is so unused to receiving love that he doesn't dare form a relationship with somebody who would love him for fear that he would not know how to react; the Hurrier secretly knows that her insatiable quest to be unconditionally and overwhelmingly loved is an unrealizable dream. From her all-or-nothing frame of reference the Hurrier inevitably ends up with nothing. When the Stiff Upper Lipper and the Hurrier describe the principal Adapted Child relationship between a couple it may be very reliably inferred that they will assure each other of extreme pain and unhappiness, which will be a reflection of the profound emotional neglect that each of them suffered in childhood.

The Try Harder and the Doormat. This is most likely to be an amicable but dreary relationship. That is, neither is likely to hurt the other, but neither will they stimulate each other to reach beyond the *narrowly unambitious and respectable* limits they impose on their lives. The Doormat is 'nice' to the Try Harder in not pressing him to achieve anything, and the Try Harder conforms in his behaviour to the Doormat's need to be 'respectable'. The worst they are likely to do to each other from time to time is for the Try Harder to think (but perhaps not even say aloud) that the Doormat is pretentious, and for the Doormat to think (but almost certainly never say) that the Try Harder is a failure.

The Try Harder and the Hurrier. The basic characteristic of this relationship is *tension.* The Try Harder is 'driven crazy' by the Hurrier and the Hurrier is made wildly impatient by the Try Harder. Each justifies his or her own Adapted Child behaviour in terms of the *provocation of the other*. The Hurrier says, 'If only he weren't so damn slow I could be calm'; the Try harder says, 'If only she'd give me some peace I could finish this.' Neither of them achieves anything positive by this dishonest projection of responsibility for their own hang-ups, but they may eventually succeed in provoking a heart attack in each other.

The Doormat and the Hurrier. From the point of view of the Hurrier, this relationship can be nearly as good for him as a relationship with a Perfectionist. Although the Perfectionist is basically more capable than the Doormat of providing the Hurrier with the profound existential control he so desperately needs, the Doormat can offer the Hurrier a great deal of *reassurance*. It is as if the Hurrier is saying, 'It's no good expecting love to last. People give it to you for a little while, but then they inevitably withdraw it and you are left abandoned and alone.' To which the Doormat replies, 'I know exactly how you feel, how frightening it is to think of being left alone. But you know it's not inevitable. So long as you are *good*, the people who love you will stay with you forever. Here, let me show you how to be good.' Through this implicit dialogue between them, the Hurrier learns how to be a Doormat and so achieves protection from the much more frightening Hurrier in him. In this relationship, the satisfaction to the Doormat derives mainly from the *reassurance* she gets that her partner's essential emotional dependence is even greater than her own.

CHAPTER ELEVEN

Friendship or Love?

We are now ready for you to decide what you want in a mate. Although all our ego states inevitably play some part in all our relationships, we very often choose our friends or lovers specifically to get the strokes we are seeking for one particular ego state. You will need to decide if this is the case for you, and, particularly, whether you are seeking *sameness or complementarity* as the central feature of the relationship between your and your mate's ego states.

When samenesses between the people involved are central to a relationship, we usually call the relationship 'friendship'. There are Parent to Parent, Adult to Adult, Free Child to Free Child, and Adapted Child to Adapted Child friendships.

When complementarity between the people involved is central to a relationship, we usually call the relationship 'love'. There is Parent to Child/Child to Parent love, Free Child to Free Child love, and Adapted Child to Adapted Child love.

This chapter is concerned with delineating the different kinds of *relationships between ego states* from which you can choose a mate whose basic needs are compatible with your own. (Chapter 11 will enable you to make sure the *contents* of your own and your mate's ego states – your messages and decisions – are also compatible.)

SAMENESS AND COMPLEMENTARITY

You are now equipped to choose a mate in the full knowledge of your wants and needs. In making your choice you need to recognize that, in broad terms, you will be selecting two different sets of characteristics:

(1) what proportions of the different ego states you want to make up the 'whole self' of your mate; more specifically, which of your ego states and which of your mate's ego states you want to predominate in the relationship.
(2) what kinds of messages and decisions you want your mate to have in each of his or her ego states.

In making these choices you are likely to be choosing either someone who *matches you* or someone who *complements you* in important ways.

Thus, in choosing what kind of distribution of energy amongst ego states you want, you may decide on *sameness*. For example:

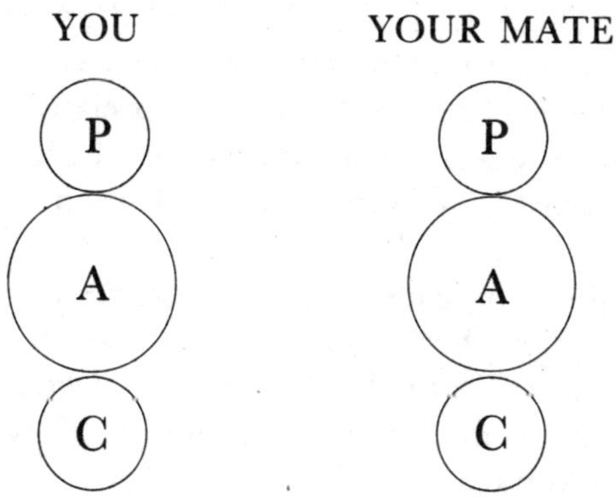

or you may decide on *complementarity*. For example:

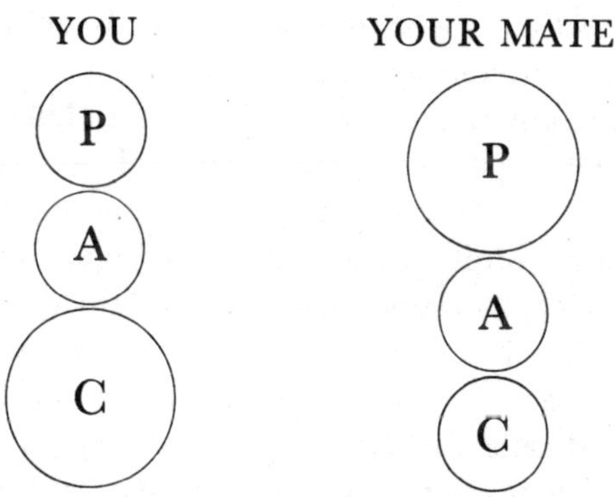

In deciding what messages and decisions you want your mate to have you need to make similar choices for sameness or complementarity. For example, you may choose such samenesses as both of you being Jewish or Roman Catholic or middle-class or Welsh nationalists (Parent samenesses); both being interested in music or politics or psychology or fossil-hunting (Adult samenesses); both enjoying gourmet food or golf or walking or parties or collecting antiques or dancing or performing in a band or . . . (permission samenesses); and, most profoundly of all, you may choose a mate for the sameness of your decisions, especially your overall assessments of what is most important in life, be it family life, material security, job satisfaction, adventure or anything else.

In choosing complementarity of messages or decisions you will be choosing the excitement and tension of opposites, with all the attendant risks of the tension degenerating from positive excitement into irreconcilable hostility. For example, 'He's a Marxist, I'm Conservative' (Parent complementarity); 'She's a physicist, I'm an artist' (Adult complementarity); 'I'm a night owl, he likes to get up at six and go to bed at ten' (Child complementarity); 'I believe in putting family togetherness first, she insists on everybody doing their own thing' (decision complementarity).

Naturally, any relationship will include elements of sameness and elements of complementarity. It would be impossible not to discern some samenesses in the individuals who make up any couple, even if only such generalities as the sameness of their nationality or their skin colouring. And complementarity inheres in the most basic fact that marriages are made out of one male and one female! However, in most of the details, the choice between complementarity and sameness is wide open, and is vitally important in determining the overall quality of the relationship you choose, as we shall see.

In general, I believe 'friendship' is the name we usually give to relationships in which samenesses between the people involved are a central feature of the relationship; and 'love' is the name we usually give to relationships in which the attraction of oppositeness is a central feature of the relationship.

The rest of this chapter is concerned with detailing the kinds of friendship or love you may decide to choose for yourself in selecting a mate, in terms of *which ego state(s) of yours and which ego state(s) of his or hers you want to predominate in the relationship*. In Chapter 12 we will go through a checklist of the *contents* of your and your prospective mate's ego states with a view to your making the choices of sameness or complementarity in your messages and decisions.

WHAT FRIENDSHIP MEANS

A friend is someone with whom we share an important part of ourselves. The part of us and the part of our friend that relate to each other are *the same in each of us*. Parent to Parent friendships are based on shared values; Adult to Adult friendships are based on shared interests; Free Child to Free Child friendships are based on shared pleasures; and Adapted Child to Adapted Child friendships are based on shared misery.

Parent to Parent friendship. Parent to Parent friendships exist between people who are united in a common cause. People doing charitable work together, sitting on a committee together, lobbying Parliament together, running a play-group together, are all enjoying Parent to Parent friendships. Having our own children is a sure-fire way of creating the opportunity for Parent to Parent friendships. Once we are mothers and fathers, looking after our children becomes a central feature of our lives, and we happily form friendships with other parents, especially with those whose children are close in age to our own, so we can compare notes on stages of child development – teething, talking, bed-wetting, learning to read, looking after teeth, discipline, etc., etc.

In many countries of the world, where marriage is seen as primarily concerned with the rearing of children, Parent to Parent compatibility between partners is considered the single most important factor making for a happy marriage.

To many people who value romantic love, this seems a pretty dull basis for marriage, but the truth is that such marriages tend to work well. The partners are very much in unison in their values and generalizations about life and, because our Parent ego state gets more important in our lives as we get older – either through having children or just as we assume more responsibilities in our work – such marriages tend to grow stronger rather than weaker with the passing of years.

Adult to Adult friendship. Adult to Adult friendships are based on companionship. Thoughtful conversation is the chief expression of such friendships, which are often made between people who are colleagues at work and enjoy their work sufficiently to pursue their interest in it even in their leisure time.

Adult to Adult marriages are often the preferred type of marriage from middle-age onwards, when the sensual Child is usually not as overwhelming of our 'whole self' as it was in youth, and the most demanding responsibilities of parenthood are also past. Adult to Adult based marriages are often found amongst childless couples who share their work, be it in business or archaeology or politics.

Free Child to Free Child friendship. Free Child to Free Child friendships are based on fun. People playing sport together, dancing together, laughing together, eating and drinking together, enjoying sex with each other, listening to music together, seeing a good film or play together, are all enjoying Free Child to Free Child friendships.

Free Child to Free Child marriages are the stuff of romantic love, since excitement, passion, sexuality and all other forms or sensuality are contained in the Child. But the Child is often fickle in the fun it seeks, so a marriage based on this compatibility runs a grave risk of not lasting long if there is no back-up compatibility between the couple's Adult and Parent ego states as well. (In this respect Free Child to Free

Child friendship is contrastable with Free Child to Free Child love, as we shall see.)

Adapted Child to Adapted Child friendship. Adapted Child to Adapted Child friendships enable us to *reaffirm our fundamental painful decisions without feeling the full brunt of the pain.* That is, friends who share our same basic decisions agree with us without our having to set things up to get negative strokes in order to prove our decisions. Thus two Perfectionists may happily agree with each other about what a disgustingly filthy housekeeper their friend, Mrs. X, is; two Stiff Upper Lippers may compare notes on the lack of discipline in schools; two Try Harders support each other in blaming circumstances beyond their control for their hardships; two Doormats enjoy having coffee with each other out of nice china cups with linen napkins; and two Hurriers probably enjoy getting drunk together.

WHAT LOVE MEANS

A person we love is someone who, in an important way, is *opposite and complementary to us.* Parent to Child/Child to Parent love is based on one person being the boss and looking after the other, who is compliant and securely cared for; Free Child to Free Child love is based on the fundamental attraction between the opposites of masculinity and femininity, and Adapted Child to Adapted Child love is based on two different personality types interacting to give each other their target negative strokes.

Parent to Child/Child to Parent love. Parent to Child/Child to Parent love finds its natural expression between children and their mothers and fathers. But many people incorporate this natural relationship of childhood into the core of their being in the form of a decision that this is the only form of 'real love'. Parent to Child/Child to Parent marriages are traditional in our culture and are constantly presented as an ideal in the vast majority of the soap operas and domestic comedies on television. Typically, the husband, as breadwinner, is Parent to his wife's need for money, to which she responds with charming Child flutteriness and intuition. But these roles are reversed when the little boy Child in the husband comes home with a cold, feeling inordinately sorry for himself, and the wife, in her Parent, tucks him up in bed with a nice hot toddy.

This type of relationship however need not be based on the trivial stereotypes so often depicted. Profoundly happy relationships may be based on this complementarity, when the roles of each partner are clearly defined, and each takes pleasure in fulfilling the dependency needs of the other as well as having his or her own dependency needs met.

The only trouble is that, although such love usually happily absorbs all the emotionality (Parent and Child) of both partners, there is usually very little objective (Adult) interaction between them, and, often, one or both of them is dissatisfied with this deficiency. Typically, the man – if he is lucky – may get strokes to his Adult through his work, but the woman's deprivation of strokes to her Adult is often a source of great unhappiness to her, which may so overwhelm her as to threaten the whole relationship. Fortunately, though, the Women's Liberation Movement has done much to draw attention to what is lacking in such relationships, with the result that most young couples today self-consciously and positively make sure that the woman's as well as the man's Adult is given its fair share of strokes.

Free Child to Free Child love. Free Child to Free Child love is like Free Child to Free Child friendship in its sensuality and joy. But it is more profound than friendship because it is aware of *oppositeness more than sameness,* and the attraction of opposites is universally the deepest and most wondrous thing we ever experience. In such love a woman feels like

Everywoman and a man feels like Everyman. Their union represents for each of them the fulfilment of the yearning of their separate, incomplete selves to be made whole. For people who know sex as the ultimate expression of this relationship, friendship sex is but a pale shadow of 'the real thing'.

Friendship sex is basically about 'having fun' together, whereas sex that expresses Free Child to Free Child love is expressing the profound complementarity between 'maleness' and 'femaleness' that exists in a unique way in each couple. (Free Child to Free Child love is not restricted to the 'Me Tarzan, you Jane' stereotype; 'masculinity' and 'femininity' are both present in the Free Child of each of us, and can relate in multitudinous ways to the 'masculinity' and 'femininity' in another. It might well be, for example, that, for a particular couple the 'femininity' in the man is in love with the 'masculinity' in the woman.)

The magic of Free Child to Free Child love cannot be made to happen. When the time and the other person are right, the Child knows with an immediacy and a sureness that neither the wise Parent nor the rational Adult can ever hope to compete with. Marriages based on this kind of love, if not contaminated by Adapted Child love – *but this is a very big If* – may be happy for a lifetime.

Adapted Child to Adapted Child love. The trouble with Adapted Child to Adapted Child love is that it masquerades so well as Free Child love. *The excitement and sureness of the Adapted Child are as convincing as the excitement and sureness of the Free Child.* Only later, does a person who falls in love from his Adapted Child realize that the excitement was about having found somebody profoundly able to give him his *negative rather than his positive target strokes.* But because of our deep compulsion to reaffirm our painful Adapted Child decisions, most relationships based on Adapted Child to Adapted Child love go on and on and on. In turn, each of the partners threatens to leave, sometimes even actually doing so, but each of them basically admits that negative strokes are better than none and the couple usually comes together again in a spirit of *Trying Hard to be happy – and failing* – and repeating the same predictable, painful, wasteful cycle over and over again.

An Adapted Child to Adapted Child relationship often masquerades as Parent to Child/Child to Parent, and these *pseudo Parent to Child/Child to Parent relationships* probably make up the vast majority of all unhappy marriages. That is, the commonest type of miserable marriage consists of the partners taking it in turns to be the Persecuting giver of negative strokes (pseudo-Parent) or the Victimized receiver of them (pseudo/Free Child).

Any of the Adapted Child personality types may be well matched in pain to any other type. Even the same types may choose to cause each other pain, although, generally speaking, we are good friends with people whose Adapted Childs match our own. However, the two particular pairs of Adapted Childs that are very commonly involved in unhappy relationships are the Stiff Upper Lipper with the Hurrier and the Stiff Upper Lipper with the Doormat.

The Stiff Upper Lipper sets things up so that he gives love in the hope of being appreciated, but proves, in the end, 'I am unloveworthy and rejected.' The Hurrier sets things up so that he rejects offers of intimacy in order to prove that the attempt to get love is futile. As was shown in Chapter 10, the Stiff Upper Lipper and the Hurrier can cause each other great pain.

The Stiff Upper Lipper longs to be given strokes without having to ask for them; the Doormat longs to be told exactly what to feel and do. In this relationship, the Stiff Upper Lipper ends up feeling unappreciated, the Doormat ends up feeling misunderstood. In Britain, the Stiff Upper Lipper (usually the man) is very commonly married to a Doormat (usually the woman) and both feel deeply stroke-deprived in their relationship.

Remember, though, the one pair of Adapted Child types that actually do each other good. This is the Perfectionist with the Hurrier. It is as if each is capable of cancelling out the other's impulses that lead to pain. The Perfectionist slows down the Hurrier and gives her a belief in life; the Hurrier jolts the Perfectionist out of his stodginess and adds the excitement of some unpredictability to his life. The Hurrier and the Perfectionist often form a stable and happy relationship.

This leads us into our final chapter, which helps you to choose a mate on the basis of finding someone whose messages and decisions are a good match or complement to your own.

CHAPTER TWELVE

Making the Choice

Choosing a mate effectively for maximum long-term happiness means using your Parent, Adult, Free Child – and even your Adapted Child – to make the choice. For every painful decision in the Adapted Child there may be as many or more joyful decisions. The painful aspects of the Adapted Child have been stressed in this book because it is awareness of these that we most often evade, but which nevertheless continue to exert their inexorable pull.

Once we have honestly and squarely faced the reality that our Adapted Child urges us to pain, there are two ways in which we can curb its power in our lives. First, by choosing to redistribute the energy amongst our ego states, giving added energy to our Parent, Adult, and Free Child in our daily lives, we can weaken the Adapted Child by starving it of energy. Secondly, we can choose to use our Adapted Child 'personality types' in positive rather than negative ways and, at the same time find positive rather than negative ways to fulfil our decisions.

Now, in terms of both *energy and content,* we are able to choose a mate freely and with true confidence that our choice will be a good one.

HOW TO AVOID HATE

Before we proceed to the final checklist that will enable you to make sure your *messages and decisions* are compatible with your prospective mate's messages and decisions – at least in the matters that are most important to you both – I would like to dispel some of the Adapted Child gloom that may have seemed to permeate this book so far.

If the power of our Adapted Child impulses to pain has been a little overstated, this overstatement has been in a good cause. Most people deny the reality of their compulsion to seek pain as well as pleasure, but this does not make their Adapted Child disappear. Not facing the Adapted Child squarely just means allowing it to be the slave driver of the rest of our 'whole selves'. Kidding ourselves that it is 'other people', 'life' or 'luck' that are responsible for our miseries, whilst we ourselves are motivated only to pure pleasure is a *delusion.* Most people *live* this delusion, just like the girl who insists, 'He must be in love with me or he wouldn't ignore me the way he does.'

If you have read this book with honesty and courage, the reward will be an ability *really to choose* a mate with the true confidence that can only exist if the Parent, the Adult and the Free Child as well as the Adapted Child decide. Remember, in choosing between alternatives, it is the Adult which enables the Child to get what it wants within the constraints of reality, and the Parent and Adult between them are capable of sound judgements, and the Parent and Child are capable of happy compromises.

As well as the pain our Adapted Child prompts us to seek, our Parent, Adult and Free Child are also there, to give us pleasure, and many people also have lots of *pleasurable decisions* written into their Adapted Child. For every decision to end up feeling worthless, unappreciated, a failure, misunderstood or futile, there are as many – or more – possibilities of decisions to love and be loved and to be an overall winner rather than an overall loser.

In the full knowledge of the realities of our Parent, Adult, Free Child and Adapted Child, we are capable of greatly diminishing the pain and increasing the pleasure of our lives, while still recognizing the essential immutability of our decisions. This can be achieved through free choice, in two ways.

(1) *Put your energy where you want it.* First, our capacity to express ourselves at all derives from the fact that we are *energy systems*. Although there are probably inborn differences between people in the total amounts of energy they have to express in life, each of us seems to have our own fixed amount. As new-born babies the total energy of our beings is contained in our Free Child, but gradually, as our Adapted Child, Adult and Parent ego states develop, our Free Child gives away some of its energy to these other ego states. The final proportions of our total energy in each of our ego states is mostly determined by how much stroking each ego state got during the course of its development. Sensibly, we chose in childhood to put most energy into the ego states we found it was easiest to get strokes for. But habitual as our childhood division of energy may have become, there is nothing to prevent us choosing to change it. If we consciously – with our Adults – decide, for example, to increase the energy of our Parent, Adult and Free Child, it is inevitable that the

expressiveness of our Adapted Child will be curtailed. There will simply be less energy left for it.

(2) *Fulfil your decisions happily.* Secondly, there is probably no 'bad' decision which cannot be turned into a 'good' decision. I knew a man with a decision to 'live a life of crime', who combined this decision happily with his permission to love fishing, becoming a river policeman. A woman with a decision, 'Men abuse me, but confronting them would make things worse – so I won't,' chose to fulfil this decision by becoming a part-time social worker amongst the down-and-outs under Waterloo Bridge – and so saved her marriage. And I have even seen a man with the horrible decision, 'Life is waiting for death,' enabled to give up his heroin addiction and find some real pleasure in life, when he found gratification of his decision through working in a mortuary. *Knowing our decisions, we are able freely to choose how to express them.*

The Perfectionist, the Stiff Upper Lipper, the Try Harder, the Doormat and the Hurrier represent the five general categories into which all painful decisions fall. Like all our individual, unique decisions, these general decisions may also find acceptable and pleasurable rather than objectionable and painful outlets. Remember that hidden amongst all the negative personality traits of the five types are some very positive Adult and Parent attributes.

The Perfectionist is an excellent organizer.
The Stiff Upper Lipper is utterly reliable.
The Try Harder is superb whenever persistence is needed.
The Doormat's flexibility makes him an excellent member of a team.
The Hurrier is extremely efficient.

Remember to stroke yourself and others for these positive attributes derived from your own and their Adapted Childs.

ADDING UP THE PROS AND CONS

Now make your choice.

In general, which type of relationship do you basically want: Parent to Parent, Adult to Adult, Child to Child or Child to Parent/Parent to Child? Make sure you and your prospective mate agree on this matter.

Are your general expectations of relationships, in terms of your birth stories, compatible?

In particular, what strokes is your Parent looking for? Is your prospective mate willing and able to provide them?

In particular, what strokes is your Adult looking for? Is your prospective mate willing and able to provide them?

In particular, what strokes is your Free Child looking for? Is your prospective mate willing and able to provide them?

What strokes to his/her Parent does your prospective mate want? Are you willing and able to provide them?

What strokes to his/her Adult does your prospective mate want? Are you willing and able to provide them?

What strokes to his/her Free Child does your prospective mate want? Are you willing and able to provide them?

Are you both realistic enough not to expect your mate to fulfil *all* your stroke needs? Make a list of all your stroke needs in order of their importance to you. Get your prospective mate to do the same. Are you both able and willing to fulfil each other's most important stroke needs? Are there areas of life where either of you is likely to feel stroke-deprived by the other? If so, make sure you both know from what other relationships or activities you will get these stroke needs met, and agree to give each other the freedom to do so.

What is your core decision about the general meaning of life? Is it compatible with your prospective mate's core decision about the general meaning of life?

What are your and your prospective mate's target negative strokes? Do you give them to each other? What are your Adapted Child types? How much pain do you cause each other? Are you both willing to talk about your Adapted Childs from Adult to Adult and with understanding and compassion help each other transform pain into pleasure?

Choose your mate with your whole self. Make judgements and compromises and find alternatives both within yourself and between the ego states of your separate selves.

A final word on the Adapted Child. Ideally, we seek to avoid completely the painful aspects of our Adapted Childs, but, because we are human, we are bound sometimes to seek and find pain as well as joy in our most intimate relationships. Rather than aiming for the unrealizable ideal of eliminating pain from your life, seek to understand it fully, be in control of it – and even enjoy it. Someone whose Adapted Child tends to feel victimized will make a compatible match with someone whose Adapted Child tends to be a bit of a persecutor. Our Adapted Child is as sexually charged as our Free Child and there is no harm in enjoying the added excitement of a little sadism and masochism, especially if we are *aware* of what we are doing and can call a halt before we escalate it into heavy-handed misery. As Ogden Nash put it, 'A little incompatibility is the spice of life, particularly if he has income and she is pattable.'

Good hunting!

GLOSSARY

ADAPTED CHILD That part of the CHILD EGO STATE which is learned, as contrasted with the FREE CHILD, which is innate. The Adapted Child is acquired mostly between the ages of about one and three, in the form of rigid rules restricting expression of the FREE CHILD. At this stage of development such rigid restrictions are necessary for the socialization and safety of the child, because her ADULT EGO STATE is not yet sufficiently developed for her to be reasonable, and her PARENT EGO STATE, which will later express care for herself and others, does not yet exist. Along with all the necessary rules that parents transmit to the Adapted Child ego states of their children, they also transmit some unnecessary constraints based on their hang-ups which, in turn, are likely to become their children's hang-ups and their children's children's hang-ups . . . until such time as the vicious cycle is broken by awareness and objective readjustment of the personality.

ADULT The EGO STATE that contains knowledge and skills. It first appears in the 'whole self' at about one year of age and grows most rapidly from then until about three years of age and again between the ages of about six and twelve, although it is capable of continued growth throughout life.

Its function in the 'whole self' is to store and assess objectively information it receives from the environment, and to make sense of life by reconciling its own information with the values of the PARENT EGO STATE and the feelings of the CHILD EGO STATE.

ALTERNATIVES The outcome of the effective collaboration of the ADULT and CHILD EGO STATES.

CHILD The EGO STATE that contains feelings and impulses. It is the only EGO STATE we are born with. At first, it is only capable of the instinctive experience and expression of overall satisfaction or overall distress, but it develops, both naturally and by conditioning, the capacity to experience and express a wide range of differentiated feelings and impulses. Its most rapid development takes place in the first three years of life.

COMPROMISE The outcome of the effective collaboration of the PARENT and CHILD EGO STATES.

CONFLICT The experience of an IMPASSE between the PARENT and CHILD EGO STATES.

CONFUSION The content of the CONTAMINATION of the PARENT and CHILD EGO STATES.

CONTAMINATION A maladaptive, pseudo-resolution of an IMPASSE between EGO STATES, in which the incompatible impulses or attitudes of the relevant EGO STATES are expressed in a single, inauthentic idea or attitude.

DECISION The sense that the ADULT EGO STATE makes of an aspect of physical or psychological reality, by reconciling and synthesizing the relevant MESSAGES received by the PARENT, ADULT and CHILD EGO STATES. Decisions fulfil the innate need of all human beings to experience life as ordered and predictable rather than arbitrary and chaotic, so, once a decision is made by an individual, he has a powerful vested interest in abiding by it. Insofar as our most fundamental decisions about life are made before the age of six, at a time when the ADULT EGO STATE's reasoning capacity is still very immature and the data it has at its disposal is very limited, we all have, amongst our decisions, some that are no longer appropriate in our grown-up lives. Nevertheless, we cling tenaciously – though often unconsciously – to our decisions, and actually changing a decision is a very difficult task indeed. However, once an individual is aware of his decisions, he has the choice of channelling even the difficult ones into healthy and adaptive rather than unhealthy and maladaptive expression.

DELUSION The content of the CONTAMINATION of the ADULT and CHILD EGO STATES.

EGO STATE One of the 'sub-selves' that go to make up the 'whole self' of every human being. These are the PARENT, the ADULT and the CHILD.

FREE CHILD That part of the CHILD EGO STATE which is innate, as contrasted with the ADAPTED CHILD, which is learned. It contains, and expresses spontaneously, feelings and impulses that are authentic and appropriate to its desires or reactions.

IMPASSE The experience of an unresolved disagreement between two EGO STATES, when they are equally energized and neither will give in or make concessions to the other.

INDECISIVENESS The experience of an IMPASSE between the PARENT and ADULT EGO STATES.

JUDGEMENT The outcome of the effective collaboration of the PARENT and ADULT EGO STATES.

MESSAGE An overt or covert transaction (usually from Mother or Father) making a powerful and lasting imprint on the EGO STATES of the growing child. Whereas ordinary communication is possible between any EGO STATE of one person and any EGO STATE of another person, a message is understood to be communicated only between the same EGO STATES of the people involved. Thus our growing PARENT EGO STATES are fed by messages from our parents' PARENT EGO STATES, our ADULT EGO STATES receive messages from their ADULT EGO STATES, and our CHILD EGO STATES receive messages from their CHILD EGO STATES.

PARENT The EGO STATE that contains values and beliefs and moral principles and generalizations about life. It is basically formed between the ages of about three and six, through explicit exhortations by our parents concerning caring for ourselves and others. In grown-up life the PARENT EGO STATE is capable of modification and growth to the extent that we may reject old values and acquire new ones as a consequence of new experiences and meeting with new, admired people. But, by and large, our PARENT EGO STATE remains committed to the principles it was taught in early childhood. Its function in the 'whole self' is to enable us automatically to behave in ways which are conducive to our own and others' well-being, including the monitoring of our FREE CHILD, by granting indulgences or imposing constraints on it according to the PARENT's own principles. In its constraining of the FREE CHILD the PARENT often looks like the ADAPTED CHILD, but the PARENT acts in accordance with general principles and may be flexible, whereas the ADAPTED CHILD is utterly rule-bound and rigid.

PERMISSION An attribute of the FREE CHILD EGO STATE which is noticeably pronounced in the 'whole self' of an individual. Although innate temperamental differences between people to some extent account for the different permissions that different people exhibit, permissions are largely created by positive STROKES given in early childhood to particular expressions of the FREE CHILD. As well as the FREE CHILD being given direct, positive STROKES (usually from Mother or Father), permissions are also developed when the child witnesses his parents in their own FREE CHILD EGO STATES which, in practice, usually amounts to his seeing them enjoying themselves. Thus if a child sees his parents *enjoying* such activities as reading, cooking, playing cards or being with friends, taking particular pleasure in these things will be included in the child's repertoire of permissions, together with the spontaneously expressed aspects of his own FREE CHILD for which his parents gave him positive STROKES.

PERSECUTOR One of the compulsive, maladaptive roles through which the ADAPTED CHILD EGO STATE may express itself. The Persecutor role is associated with an inauthentic feeling of, 'Now I've got you, you son-of-a-bitch!

PREJUDICE The content of the contamination of the PARENT and ADULT EGO STATES.

RESCUER One of the compulsive, maladaptive roles through which the ADAPTED CHILD EGO STATE may express itself. The Rescuer role is associated with an inauthentic feeling of self-righteousness.

STROKES A stroke is any act of recognition given by one person to another. Our need for and quest for strokes is continuous and life-long; when positive strokes – which make us feel good – are not available, we would prefer to get negative strokes – which make us feel bad – than receive no strokes at all, that is be ignored. At birth we are only capable of appreciating the most fundamental strokes, such as actual physical contact with another human being, but gradually we learn to value as strokes a wide variety of symbolic substitutes for actual physical contact, from the slightly valued nod of a passing acquaintance to the profoundly gratifying 'I love you.' The strokes – both POSITIVE and NEGATIVE – that we were often given in childhood by our parents are the strokes that we are most likely to seek and to get from other people for the rest of our lives. These are called our TARGET STROKES. We each have our own POSITIVE TARGET STROKES – which make us feel especially good about ourselves – and our own NEGATIVE TARGET STROKES – which make us feel especially bad about ourselves.

STRUGGLE The experience of an IMPASSE between the ADULT and CHILD EGO STATES.

VICTIM One of the compulsive, maladaptive roles through which the ADAPTED CHILD EGO STATE may express itself. The Victim role is associated with an inauthentic feeling of helplessness.